# Love and Faith After 5D

## Spirituality Beyond Religion

## Additional Books by Sonia A. Tolson

*The Soul of Remembering:*
*Tools, Truths, And Teachings for the Returning Soul*

*No, You Are Not Losing Your Mind:*
*Tools for Your Spiritual Awakening*

*Companion to the Soul of Remembering:*
*A Guided Journey or Integration, Reflection, and Soulstream Activation*

*Crystalline Allies:*
*Partnering with the Living Light of the Mineral Kingdom*

*Divorcing a Soul Fractal:*
*Reclaiming Your Flame*

*Soulstream Homecoming Guide:*
*A Path to Welcoming Your Soul Fractal Home*

Sold in online bookstores.

# Love and Faith After 5D

*Spirituality Beyond Religion*

## Sonia A. Tolson

Celestial Weaver Publishing
Tucson, Arizona

Copyright © 2025 Sonia A. Tolson
All Rights Reserved.

No part of this publication may be reproduced, stored in a retrieval system, or transmitted in any form or by any means – electronic, mechanical, photocopying, recording, or otherwise – without the prior written permission of the author, except in the case of brief quotations embodied in critical articles or reviews.

This is a work of spiritual nonfiction. The experiences, transmissions, and interpretations within are shared in the spirit of soul remembrance and personal truth. While every effort has been made to present these teachings with accuracy and integrity, the author makes no guarantees of results and encourages readers to use discernment and inner resonance as their guide.

E-book ISBN:
Paperback ISBN:
Library of Congress:

Cover design and interior formatting by:
The Soul of Remembering Design Team

For permission, inquiries, or rights requests,
Please contact:
Celestial Weaver Publishing
CelestialWeaverPublishing@gmail.com

Printed in the United States of America, 1st Edition

# Dedication

To God (Source, Abba, the great I AM, Great Spirit)
The infinite love and light in which all things live, move, and have their being.
May these words reflect even a small spark of Your eternal truth.

And to my beloved family —
Greg, Makayla, Zachary, and Allison —
thank you for walking beside me in this life with patience, love, and strength.
You are my most excellent teachers and the living reminders of why faith and love endure.

# Acknowledgments

First and always, I give thanks to the Source of all, the eternal wellspring of love and truth, for guiding my steps, sustaining my spirit, and filling these pages with light.

To my family, Greg, Makayla, Zachary, and Allison: thank you for your patience, encouragement, and love through every stage of this journey. You have been my grounding and my greatest joy.

To the many friends, readers, and fellow seekers who have walked beside me, shared your stories, and offered encouragement: you are part of the living tapestry of this work. Your presence reminds me that none of us walks alone.

And finally, to every soul leaving behind old beliefs or stepping cautiously toward new truths: this book is for you. May you find comfort, courage, and clarity as you discover love and faith beyond the walls of religion.

# About the Author

Sonia writes with a heart for seekers, those who are leaving behind religion or longing for something deeper than doctrine. Her work bridges the gap between traditional faith and expansive spirituality, offering a path of love, unity, and authentic connection with Source.

Through her Soulstream Series and companion works, Sonia shares wisdom gathered from a lifetime of questioning, searching, and remembering. Her books invite readers into a space of healing, self-discovery, and freedom, encouraging them to cultivate their own direct relationship with the Divine, free from fear, judgment, or limitation.

She lives in the breathtakingly beautiful Sonoran Desert with her husband, Greg, where the vast skies and quiet landscapes inspire her writing. Together, they share life with their children — Makayla, Allison, and Zachary — and a lively flock of hens and rescue dogs.

When she isn't writing, Sonia finds joy in tending her crystal room, walking in the desert, and connecting with readers who, like her, are ready to embrace spirituality beyond religion.

# A Note to the Reader

This book is written for seekers of every kind, whether you come from a religious background, a scientific mindset, or a mixture of both.

You don't have to believe in reincarnation, angels, or even a higher consciousness to find meaning here. What matters is your openness to explore love, faith, and spirituality beyond the limits of fear and division.

Some people refer to the source of life as "God." Others refer to it as "Source," "Spirit," "the field," or even "the energy matrix," which science is beginning to describe. Whatever you name it, or whether you name it at all, the truth is that love, compassion, and unity are universal experiences. They belong to everyone.

The reflections and practices in these pages are not meant to persuade you into a new system of belief. They are invitations to experiment for yourself. To notice what shifts in your heart when you practice stillness, forgiveness, compassion, or openness.

Whether you see these shifts as spiritual, psychological, or energetic doesn't matter. What matters is that they bring healing, peace, and a sense of connection.

Take what resonates with you, leave what doesn't, and allow your own experience to be your teacher.

This is a book about love. And love does not demand belief; it only asks to be lived.

# Table of Contents

Dedication

Acknowledgments

About the Author

A Note to the Reader

Introduction..................................................................1

1. Why We Reach for a Higher Power............................3
2. The Birth of Religions.................................................11
3. When Dogma Entered.................................................17
4. The Core Teaching is Love.........................................23
5. Compassion as Practice..............................................29
6. Mystics Across Traditions..........................................35
7. Sacred Rituals: The Universal Language...................41
8. When Faith Hurts........................................................47
9. Wars in God's Name....................................................53
10. Reclaiming the Good..................................................59
11. Spirituality Without Borders.....................................65
12. Love as the Common Denominator..........................71

13. Living Spiritually in Modern Life............................77

14. Practices for Universal Connection.........................93

15. The Thread Continues..........................................101

16. Why Does God Allow Suffering..............................107

17. Who is God?........................................................117

18. Glimpses Beyond the Veil.....................................127

19. Love in a 3D World..............................................137

20. Living Abundance in 5D........................................145

21. The Future is Watching: Love Beyond Division........157

Appendices

- Appendix A: Sacred Echoes............................................163

- Appendix B: The Psalm of Trust......................................181

Epilogue: Remembering Love...........................................187

Closing Blessing............................................................189

# Introduction

For many, religion has been both a comfort and a cage. It has offered a sense of belonging, meaning, and structure — but often at the cost of freedom, authenticity, and unconditional love. Doctrines of fear and judgment have deeply wounded some of us. Others never entered the doors of religion but still felt the pressure of its shadow in our culture and families.

This book is written for both. For those leaving behind religion and for those who sense there must be more before they ever step inside it. It is not a rejection of faith but a re-centering of faith where it belongs — in love, in trust, and in direct connection with Source.

We are living in a time of awakening. Old structures are falling away, and humanity is being invited to move beyond 3D — the dense world of separation, duality, and fear — into a higher way of living where love, unity, and compassion are the guiding forces. This is not abstract philosophy. It is the daily practice of remembering who we truly are: divine beings having a human experience.

In these pages, you will find reflections, transmissions, and practices meant to help you:
- Release the fear-based patterns of 3D consciousness.
- Reclaim your faith as trust in the infinite love of Source.
- Live in the vibration of love, unity, and freedom beyond dogma.

This is not a book of rules, but an invitation. An invitation to step into your birthright as a soul — free, whole, and deeply loved.

May you read with an open heart. May these words stir your remembrance. And may you discover that after 3D, love and faith are not lost; they are finally found.

# Chapter 1

## Why We Reach for a Higher Power

From the first firelit nights to the neon hum of modern cities, one question has traveled with us: Who placed me here, and why?

Every people, in every age, has answered in their own language. Some looked up at the stars and named them gods. Others felt the wind move through canyon walls and whispered to the unseen. Still others told stories of a great Parent, a Source of all light, who poured life into clay and called it good.

We reach for a Higher Power because we ache for belonging.
We reach for a Higher Power because life is both too beautiful and too brutal to carry alone.
We reach for a Higher Power because something in us remembers where we came from.

# The Human Need for a Higher Power

## A "God-Shaped Void"
Many spiritual perspectives suggest that humans are created with an inner emptiness that can only be filled by a Higher Power. This longing drives us to search beyond ourselves, reminding us that no possession, relationship, or achievement can satisfy the deepest hunger of the soul.

## Comfort and Strength in Hardship
Life is filled with seasons of grief, uncertainty, and struggle. In those moments, people instinctively reach toward the Sacred for comfort, strength, and solace. Whether standing at a graveside, praying in a hospital waiting room, or sitting in silence at the end of a long day, the human heart instinctively turns to a Higher Power as a source of refuge.

## Purpose and Meaning
The search for a Higher Power is also a search for meaning. In the face of suffering, mortality, and the unknown, we long for assurance that our lives matter and that there is purpose woven into chaos. Reaching upward offers a compass in the fog, a reminder that our stories are part of something larger.

# Spiritual Hunger and Longing

## A Thirst Beyond the Physical
The longing for connection with a Higher Power is often described as a deep spiritual hunger and thirst, an ache as real as any physical need. Until it is met with divine

presence, a person may feel restless, unsatisfied, or incomplete.

## Seeking a Higher Consciousness
This longing pulls us to seek, to be near, to listen, to be transformed. As Billy Graham once observed, people hunger not merely for religion, but for relationship, for a living connection with a presence greater than themselves, whether called Higher Power, Higher Consciousness, or Source.

## **Benefits of Seeking a Higher Power**

### Guidance and Wisdom
Turning toward a Higher Consciousness opens a pathway to understanding life's complexities. This wisdom offers clarity in decision-making, grounding in uncertainty, and direction in times of confusion.

### Peace and Fulfillment
Beyond guidance, many discover in a Higher Power a peace that surpasses understanding. This inner stillness does not ignore suffering, but transforms it, allowing the soul to rest even in the midst of storms.

### Empowerment and Transformation
To reach for a Higher Power is also to be changed. Divine connection reshapes the heart, deepens compassion, strengthens character, and awakens the courage to live with authenticity and love. It is through this transformation that individuals grow to reflect more of the sacred image.

## The Universal Longing

Anthropologists, poets, and prophets agree: the human heart is wired for wonder. From the caves of Lascaux to the psalms of David, humanity's first instinct has been to worship.

- Not because we are weak, but because we are aware.
- Not because we are blind, but because we see too much to make sense of.
- Not because we are ignorant, but because knowledge alone cannot hold the ache for eternity.

Across cultures and ages, sacred stories repeat: creation myths, figures of wisdom, laws for harmony, and rituals that bind communities together. The forms differ, but the impulse is the same.

## Beyond Names and Forms

Not everyone who lights a candle or lays out crystals believes in God. Some turn from the very Word because of wounds inflicted by religion, or because the image of God they were given no longer rings true. Yet even in this turning, the reaching remains.

Tarot cards, pendulums, meditation practices, rituals with earth and sky — these are not proof of belief in a deity, but they are proof of longing. A longing to listen more deeply, to find guidance, to touch the unseen currents that move beneath the surface of life.

Whether we call it a Higher Power, Higher Consciousness, Spirit, the Universe, or simply intuition, the human heart still yearns for connection. The outward tools may differ, but the inner impulse is the same: to quiet the noise, to find meaning, to know that we are not alone.

This is love without borders, the recognition that every seeker, no matter their path, carries the same flame of longing. What matters is not the tool in the hand, but the spark in the heart.

## Archetypes of the Divine

Throughout history, humanity has given shape to the longing for the Sacred through familiar roles:

- The Mother who nourishes and protects (Isis, Mary, Shakti, Pachamama).
- The Father who guides, disciplines, and provides (Zeus, Yahweh, Odin, Brahma).
- The Child who embodies innocence, renewal, and promise (Krishna, Horus, Christ).
- The Teacher or Sage who points the way home (Yeshua, Buddha, Confucius, indigenous elders).

We imagine the Higher Power as family, as Creator, as guide—because love is easier to grasp than infinity.

## The Spark Beneath

Strip away the names, the rituals, the scriptures, and what remains?

A pulse. A spark. A flame in the center of the chest.

It is the part of us that senses we belong to something larger, kinder, older than the world's cruelties. It is the same pulse that drives a monk to silence, a mother to prayer, a child to sing to the stars.

This is why we reach:
Not only to explain the cosmos, but to soothe the loneliness of being human.

## Journaling Invitation

- When did I first feel a longing for something beyond myself?

- Was it in beauty, in grief, in fear, or in wonder?

- If I gave that longing a shape today, what would it look like?

# Chapter 2

## The Birth of Religions

Religion is memory wrapped in story. It is humanity's first library, our first attempt to explain thunder and death, justice and love, the spark of birth and the silence of the grave.

When tribes grew into nations and stories traveled farther than firelight, the need arose for structure. Belief became a system. The mystery became an institution. And religion was born.

### Stories as Mirrors

Every religion begins with a story:

- A garden and a tree.
- A mountain where laws are given in fire and smoke.
- A prince who leaves his palace to sit beneath a fig tree.
- A wandering tribe that finds a promised land.
- A shepherd who hears the voice of God in the desert wind.

These stories are mirrors. They reflect the struggles of their people: survival, hunger, oppression, exile, and longing for justice. They are also maps, guiding hearts toward courage, compassion, or trust in something greater than kings.

## The Context of Culture

The setting matters:

- In desert lands, God is water, cloud, and rain.
- In agrarian valleys, God is fertility, grain, and harvest.
- In the high mountains, God is storm, thunder, and sky.

Each culture gave its sacred story the shape of its landscape. Religion became not only a path to the Divine but a way to hold the environment, the seasons, and the fragile balance of survival.

To belong to a religion was to belong to a people. Faith was the glue that held the community together, and often the only protection against chaos.

## From Fluid to Fixed

At first, the stories were fluid, passed from one person to another: sung, chanted, and told by elders. But as writing spread, myths became scriptures, and oral truth became written law.

With writing came permanence. With permanence came authority.

And with authority came hierarchy: priests, scribes, interpreters.

The fluid became fixed. The mystery became codified.

And while this preserved wisdom, it also sowed the seeds of dogma.

## The Gift and the Burden

The birth of religions gave humanity both a gift and a burden:

- The gift: stories carried across centuries, a sense of belonging, an anchor in the storm.
- The burden: the spark of freedom encased in stone, the danger of forgetting that story is a symbol, not a cage.

Religion, at its best, is a bridge to God.
Religion, at its worst, is a wall between one another.

Long before churches and creeds, the word *Christ* meant "the anointed one." It was a title, not a surname, a recognition of someone who had awakened to their divine nature and lived it fully.

Christ Consciousness is not limited to one teacher or era. It is a living frequency of love and unity present in all beings. When you remember that you and Source are one, and when you act from compassion instead of fear, you embody Christ Consciousness.

This is the more profound truth hidden behind centuries of doctrine: the "second coming" is not an external event but an internal awakening. It is each of us allowing the anointed self, the soul lit by Source, to take the lead in our daily lives. In this sense, every seeker is invited to be a "Christ" in their own sphere, not by claiming a title but by radiating unconditional love.

## Journaling Invitation
- What sacred story shaped my early faith?

- Did that story comfort me, frighten me, or both?

- If I could tell my own story of creation today, what would it sound like?

# Chapter 3

## When Dogma Entered

At first, the stories were wide as rivers. They flowed from mouth to mouth, carried in song, painted on cave walls, whispered by elders at the edge of firelight. The mystery was alive, shifting, shimmering, belonging to all.

But when the stories were pressed into stone and scroll, when priests began to guard what once belonged to the people, something shifted. What had been fluid became fixed. What had been for all was fenced for some.

## From Unity to Division

The golden thread was never meant to divide. Source has always been inclusive: all peoples, all tongues, all children of earth gathered in the same love.

But men, frightened of chaos, hungry for power, began to slice the thread into borders:
- "Us" and "them."
- "Believer" and "heretic."

- "Pure" and "unclean."

The very act of dividing went against the heart of Source, who breathes only wholeness. Division is not divine, but a projection of 3D duality, the illusion that separateness is real.

## When Power Hijacked the Story

Religion in its pure form was never meant to be a tool of control. Yet as kingdoms rose, rulers and priests discovered that the story could be harnessed to maintain order. Fear-based dogma was born. Obey or be cursed, conform or be cast out.

The sacred impulse was hijacked. What was once a path to inclusion became a system of exclusion, drawing lines of power that determined who was inside and who was outside the circle of belonging.

## Echoes from Egypt

Egypt offers a striking example. After the fall of Atlantis, many sought refuge along the Nile, bringing fragments of ancient knowledge, including astronomy, sacred geometry, and healing practices that utilized sound and light. The walls of temples and tombs still bear the images: beings with elongated skulls, animal-headed figures, crafts descending from the skies.

For the people of the time, these were not distant myths. They were rulers, teachers, and visitors whose knowledge surpassed human capacity. In time, awe turned into worship, and worship hardened into religion. Pharaohs claimed a divine right, and priesthoods guarded secrets that were once shared freely.

Egypt reminds us how wisdom can calcify into dogma. What may have been living contact with advanced beings, whether Atlantean survivors, star visitors, or both, became enshrined as a rigid hierarchy. Carvings in stone preserved memory, but when guarded by fear and power, even memory could be used to control.

## Fear as a Tool

When leaders sought obedience, they often resorted to instilling fear.
- Fear of exile.
- Fear of hell.
- Fear of a Higher Power imagined more as a harsh judge than as a loving parent.

Fear made people compliant, but it also made them small. It taught them to shrink from one another, to measure worth by belonging to the right side of the line.

Yet no true Source would create in love only to divide in hate.

## Dogma as Distorted Love

In 3D, even love can be distorted; turned into attachment, fear, or possession. Dogma often wore the mask of love, demanding obedience in the name of care. But love that punishes is not love; love that excludes is not love. These distortions reveal fear masquerading as devotion.

True love is expansive, not restrictive. It invites, rather than coerces. It frees, rather than binds.

## The Direct Connection

At the heart of every soul is a direct line to Source, no priest or gatekeeper required. Rituals may assist, teachers may guide, but the spark belongs to all. Dogma blurred this truth, convincing people that they were unworthy or incapable of approaching the Divine directly.

But the truth remains: each of us carries within the very presence we seek. The cathedral is the heart; the altar is awareness; the prayer is love itself.

## The Plan of Inclusion

Every religion in its purest teaching whispers the same truth:
- We are one.
- We are loved.
- We are called to love in return.

Dogma fractured this unity, but the thread is still unbroken. When the dividing walls crumble, what remains is the same song that began at the dawn of time: not us versus them, but all of us together, in Source.

For if Source is in all, and all is Source, then division is impossible. Us versus them would mean Source turning against itself, and love does not make war on love. The truth has always been unity, and the invitation has always been that of belonging.

## Journaling Invitation

- Where have I seen "us versus them" in religion, culture, or even in my own thinking?

- How would my life change if I believed Source includes everyone?

- What stories from history — Egypt, Sumer, or my own lineage — still shape how I see the Sacred today?

- Where have I mistaken fear for love?

- What small act could I take today that embodies inclusion instead of division?

# Chapter 4

## The Core Teaching is Love

At the heart of every religion, beneath layers of ritual and rule, one teaching shines with the same brilliance: Love.

From the Maxims of Ptahhotep in ancient Egypt, reminding us to "be kind while you live, for what matters after death is how you treated others," to the Torah's command to love your neighbor, to Christ's commandment of love, to the Buddha's call for compassion, to the Tao Te Ching's teaching that the greatest virtue is to live in harmony, and to the Sikh teaching that where there is love, God is revealed, the golden thread is unmistakable.

Love is not a sidebar.

It is the essence.

## Love as the Source

If Source is in all, then love is the current that moves through creation. It is not earned. It is not withheld. It is the native language of the soul. When we return to love, we return to our origin.

In 3D reality, this love often appears distorted. Attachment may masquerade as devotion, fear as protection, need as intimacy. But these are shadows of love, not love itself. True love is unconditional, expansive rather than possessive, freeing rather than binding. It is the steady vibration of Source flowing through all beings, regardless of belief, tribe, or story.

## Love in Action

Love is not sentiment alone. It is practice.

It feeds the hungry, shelters the wanderer, forgives the enemy, tends the sick. Every tradition, in its purest heart, calls its people to embody love not in words, but in deeds.

Those who have touched the threshold of death in near-death experiences often return with one central message: they were immersed in a love so vast, so unconditional, that it could not be compared to anything on earth. This love did not ask what they believed or how they lived, it simply embraced. Mystical encounters affirm what sacred texts declare: love is the essence of reality.

## Love Beyond Borders

Religions sometimes narrowed love, teaching it only for the tribe, the believer, the chosen. But love cannot be confined. It is borderless. When extended only to some, it withers. When extended to all, it multiplies.

Division is the illusion of 3D, whispering that separation is real. Love dissolves that illusion. It does not bargain, divide, or withdraw. It simply radiates, like the sun shining on all without preference. When love is allowed to flow beyond borders, it heals the fractures of culture, religion, and fear, reminding us that unity has always been our truth.

## The Christed Heart

To live in love is to awaken to what mystics call Christ Consciousness: the awareness that we and Source are one. This is not limited to one teacher or time. It is a frequency of compassion and unity that any soul may embody. The invitation is to allow the Christed heart within us to take the lead, not by claiming a title, but by radiating unconditional love. In this way, the 'second coming' is not an external arrival but an internal awakening to love without limits.

## The Heart's Reminder

Strip away every scripture, every temple, every name of God, and what remains is love. It is the one teaching no religion can erase, because it was written first, not on tablets of stone, but in the human heart.

## Journaling Invitation

- Where in my life have I most clearly experienced love as sacred?

- Do I sometimes limit love to 'my people' and how might I widen the circle?

- When have I mistaken attachment or fear for love? What did I learn from that?




- Have I glimpsed unconditional love in a mystical experience, dream, or moment of grace?

- What small act of love today could ripple farther than I imagine?

# Chapter 5

## Compassion as Practice

If love is the essence, compassion is its expression. Love lives in the heart; compassion moves through the hands.

Across traditions, compassion is more than kindness. It is the recognition of shared humanity, the truth that your suffering is my suffering, your joy is my joy. To practice compassion is to honor the unity Source has written into all life.

## Compassion in the Traditions

- In Buddhism, compassion (*karuṇā*) is paired with wisdom, the wings that carry awakening.
- In Christianity, compassion is lived in service: feeding the hungry, visiting the sick, welcoming the stranger.
- In Hinduism, compassion (*dayā*) flows from the recognition of the divine in all beings.
- In Indigenous traditions, compassion is woven into kinship: all are relatives, deserving care.

Though the language varies, the call is the same: to let love move beyond feeling and become action.

## Compassion as Courage

Compassion is not always easy. It requires stepping toward pain when instinct says to step away. It asks us to meet even the difficult, the stranger, the enemy, with dignity.

In the density of 3D reality, compassion may feel risky. Survival instinct tells us to guard, to withdraw, to protect only our own. But compassion calls us higher. To practice compassion is to act with courage, to choose unity over fear, to open the heart where it most wants to close.

## Compassion Beyond Death

Those who return from near-death experiences often describe being met not with condemnation, but with overwhelming compassion. They recall their lives reviewed not as a trial, but as a gentle unveiling, their mistakes shown through the lens of love, not judgment.

Such accounts suggest that compassion is not only an earthly practice but a cosmic principle. It is woven into the very structure of existence, surrounding us in life, death, and beyond.

## Compassion as Bridge

Compassion is the antidote to division.

Where fear draws lines — us versus them, believer versus unbeliever — compassion steps across.

Compassion recognizes the spark of Source in every being and treats no one as disposable.

To practice compassion is to build bridges where walls have been raised. It is to see beyond the illusion of separation and act from the more profound truth of unity.

## The Ripple Effect

Compassion multiplies.

A single act, a meal offered, a listening ear, a moment of forgiveness, ripples outward.

The one who receives compassion is more likely to extend it. In this way, compassion is the quiet revolution capable of softening even the hardest divisions.

## The Christed Gesture

Every act of compassion, however small, is Source flowing through us.

This is what mystics call Christ Consciousness: not an abstract doctrine, but <u>the lived radiance of love</u>.

When we tend the hurting, forgive the failing, or uplift the weary, we allow the Christed heart within us to act in the world.

Compassion is therefore not only kindness, it is incarnation. It is love taking form through our hands, our words, our choices.

## Living Compassion Daily

Compassion need not be grand to be sacred.

It lives in simple acts: holding the door, smiling at the weary cashier, speaking gently when frustration rises.

Small mercies stitch the world back together, thread by thread. In this way, compassion is both ordinary and extraordinary: accessible in every moment, yet capable of transforming the world.

## Journaling Invitation

- When have I received compassion that changed me?

- Where am I being called to show compassion that feels difficult?

- How might my compassion build a bridge across a divide in my life?

- Do I sense that compassion is not only human but divine — present even beyond death?

- What small act of compassion could I offer today?

# Chapter 6

## Mystics Across Traditions

Every religion has its mystics, those who see beyond the surface of ritual and glimpse the heart of the Divine. They are poets, dreamers, saints, sages. Their words echo across centuries, carrying the fragrance of union.

## Voices of the Mystics

- In Christianity, **Teresa of Ávila** spoke of the soul as an interior castle, every room leading deeper into God's love.
- In Sufism, **Rumi** sang of the Beloved who is closer than breath, the wine that intoxicates the soul.
- In Buddhism, **Milarepa's** songs rose from mountain caves, praising emptiness as radiant fullness.
- In Hinduism, **Mirabai** sang her love for Krishna with longing that burned brighter than fear.

- In Indigenous traditions, **shamans, seers, and elders** entered vision quests, meeting the Spirit in wind, stone, and fire.
- In Christianity, **John of the Cross** wrote of the Dark Night, where love strips away all illusions until only union with the Divine remains.
- In Christianity, **Julian of Norwich** heard in her visions the tender assurance: *"All shall be well, and all shall be well, and all manner of thing shall be well."*
- In Christianity, **Hildegard of Bingen** beheld the Living Light, radiant visions of creation suffused with God's love.
- In India, the poet-saint **Kabir** declared that the Beloved cannot be confined to a temple or a mosque, for the Divine dwells within every heart.
- In Sufi devotion, **Rabia al-Adawiyya** spoke of a love for God that is free of fear and free of reward, love for love's sake alone.
- In Lakota vision, **Black Elk** revealed the sacred hoop, where all beings are one circle woven together by Spirit.

Though they spoke in different tongues, their message was one: Love is not distant. The Holy is within and around us, waiting to be known.

**The Mystic's Path**

Mystics are often misunderstood. Their passion unsettles the comfortable. Their intimacy with the Divine makes institutions uneasy. Many were silenced, exiled, or even killed. Yet their words endure, because they ring with truth.

Mystics remind us that religion is not meant to end in dogma but to begin in direct experience. They call us to taste for ourselves what cannot be contained in creed: the sweetness of union, the fire of love, the stillness of presence.

In 3D reality, where love is so easily distorted into fear or control, mystics become clear channels. They pierce the fog and point to what is eternal. Their lives are reminders that clarity is possible even in a world of distortion.

## Modern Mystical Experiences

Mystical experience is not only the domain of saints in history. Today, countless near-death and out-of-body experiences describe the same truths: souls enveloped in light, immersed in unconditional love, freed from time and fear. These modern testimonies echo the voices of ancient mystics, affirming that the essence of the Sacred is still accessible, still present.

The mystic's song continues in the language of those who return from the edge: we are loved, we are one, and we are more than this body.

## Mystics Beyond Earth

Some wisdom-bearers come not from our own cultures, but from beyond Earth. Ancient carvings and star myths suggest contact with beings whose knowledge exceeded human ability. In modern times, messages from higher-dimensional guides carry the same themes as human mystics: unity, compassion, remembrance of Source.

Whether we call them angels, star teachers, or future kin, their role mirrors that of the mystics: to remind us that love is our origin and unity our destiny.

## Mysticism for All

Mysticism is not reserved for saints or sages. It is available to every soul. When we are fully present, in prayer, in nature, in the gaze of another, we touch the same truth the mystics sang.

The path is open to all who seek with sincerity.

In a divided world, mysticism becomes medicine. It dissolves us-versus-them by drawing us into the experience of oneness.

To taste even a drop of that unity is to know that no separation is real, and love is the foundation beneath all appearances.

## Journaling Invitation

- Whose mystical writings or teachings have most spoken to my heart?
- Have I ever touched a moment of union with something greater?

- What practices help me become more open to mystical experience?

- Do I sense mysticism in modern experiences — like NDEs, OBEs, or moments of timeless love?

- Am I open to wisdom beyond Earth, if it carries the same essence of love and unity?

# Chapter 7
## Sacred Rituals: The Universal Language

Though religions differ in doctrine, their rituals often look remarkably alike. Across cultures and centuries, humanity has employed rhythm, symbol, and ceremony to bridge the gap between the visible and the invisible.

**The Common Rituals**

- Prayer: words spoken, whispered, or sung to the Divine.
- Fasting: the body's hunger turned into devotion.
- Chanting: vibration carrying intention beyond language.
- Pilgrimage: the journey to a sacred place that mirrors the inner journey of the soul.
- Silence: emptying the noise so presence can be heard.
- Offerings: gifts of food, flowers, or incense to honor the Sacred.
- Dance and Fire: movement and flame used to awaken joy, courage, and remembrance.

Though the names and forms differ, the essence is the same: rituals bring us into alignment with the Holy.

## The Power of the Body

Rituals matter because they involve the body. Bowing, kneeling, standing, singing, walking, these are ways of teaching the body what the soul already knows: we belong to something greater. Breathwork, movement, and stillness all carry wisdom. Through ritual, faith becomes embodied, not just believed.

## Rituals as Memory

Rituals also carry memory. Lighting a candle today connects us with every ancestor who lit a flame in devotion. Chanting ancient words places us in a river of countless voices. A circle dance echoes steps traced on the earth for millennia.

Ritual binds us not only to the Divine, but to all who have walked the path before us. Each gesture becomes a thread in a tapestry woven across generations, reminding us that we are never alone.

## The Risk of Ritual

When ritual becomes an empty habit, its meaning fades. Performed without presence, ritual can become performance, a simulation of devotion rather than an opening to it. In 3D, this distortion is common: bodies move, words are spoken, but the heart remains untouched.

Yet when approached with intention, ritual becomes a living language of love. The same prayer, spoken with a heart awake, becomes new every time. Ritual is alive when consciousness is alive within it.

## Ritual as Bridge, Not Barrier

Rituals can either divide or unite.

At their worst, they are used to mark insiders and outsiders, separating one community from another.

At their best, they become bridges, spaces where people of different paths can find common ground in shared reverence.

Lighting a candle, offering a prayer, or walking in silence need no borders. They remind us that beyond names and forms, the impulse is the same: to remember our Source.

## Ritual as Preparation

Those who have crossed the threshold in near-death experiences often say that ritual is not needed in higher realms. There, love and presence are immediate. Yet here on earth, rituals help prepare the heart. They clear the noise of the mind, attune the body, and open space for remembrance.

In this way, rituals are not the destination but the doorway, preparing us to receive what is already within.

## The Heart of Ritual

Source needs no ritual.

Yet humanity creates ritual as a way to focus attention and intention. It is not the form itself that holds power, but the consciousness poured into it.

A ritual performed with fear becomes bondage; a ritual performed with love becomes liberation.

The heart of ritual is intention. When love directs the action, the simplest gesture, a breath, a bow, a flame, becomes holy.

## The Universal Language

Sacred rituals are humanity's way of saying: we remember.

We remember our Source, our unity, our dependence on love. In this sense, ritual is a universal language that every soul can understand, regardless of the name they call the Holy.

## Journaling Invitation

- Which rituals have been most meaningful in my life?

- Have I ever experienced a ritual that felt empty — and what was missing?

- How does intention shift the way I experience ritual?

- Can I see ritual as a bridge to others, even across traditions?

- What simple ritual could I create today to remind me of love's presence?

# Chapter 8

## When Faith Hurts

For many, religion has been a place of comfort, a guiding light in darkness. But for others, it has been a source of wounds: shame, exclusion, fear, and even trauma. When faith is filtered through distortion, it can leave scars instead of blessings. To heal, we must name these wounds honestly and remember that the essence of Source has never been what harmed us.

## The Wounds of Dogma

When rules replace love, faith can wound instead of heal.

Dogma has told some they are unworthy because of who they love, what they believe, or the questions they dared to ask. Instead of opening doors, religion has sometimes shut them, leaving seekers outside in the cold.

The distortion arises from what some ancient texts warned against: making an idol of our own fear and calling it God. As the Confederation of Planets has reminded us, the Creator never ordained suffering as punishment. What we call "religious wounds" are not decrees from the Divine, but projections of human frailty, stories written into doctrine by those who mistook power for truth. When rules masquerade as love, the soul can feel shackled rather than free.

## The Weight of Shame

Shame is one of the most profound wounds faith can inflict.

It whispers, 'You are not enough. You are unclean. You are unworthy of love.' This voice, claimed as God's, can echo for a lifetime.

But shame is not the voice of Source. Source has always spoken of belonging.

Near-death experiencers often return from glimpsing the higher realms with a stunning realization: in the life review, the only true measure is love, how much was given and received.

There is no tally of sins, no ledger of failures.

There is compassion, forgiveness, and understanding.

To those who have been told they were broken beyond repair, this truth dismantles the lie. Shame is a human echo; Source's voice has only ever been, 'You are my beloved.'

## The Exile of Difference

Religions have often cast out those who are different: women with voices too strong, men who loved men, seekers who doubted aloud. In the name of purity, whole groups were exiled. Yet exclusion runs against the very nature of Source, who is endlessly inclusive.

Separation itself is the grand illusion of the third dimension. As Meera of the Pleiadian High Council explains, division is not reality; it is a mirage sustained by the belief in 'us versus them.' Every exile, every gate locked against the 'other,' is ultimately humanity's trance of duality playing itself out.

But Source never turned away. Beyond the illusion, there are no outsiders. We are all rays of the same sun.

## The Courage to Name the Hurt

To heal, we must first name the wound.

Pretending it did not happen only deepens the silence.

When survivors of religious harm share their stories, they reclaim power. Their voices remind us that God does not belong to gatekeepers.

Love cannot be fenced.

As Tia of Arcturus has shared, true prayer is not about pleading with an external authority, but about merging with the flow of the Source. In this flow, the illusions of shame, fear, and exile dissolve.

To name the hurt is to step out of the trance of fear and into the remembrance of unity.

When we bear witness to our own scars, we begin to see them not as marks of divine rejection, but as catalysts that call us home to love.

**Moving Beyond Wounds**

Religion, at its purest, is meant to point toward the infinite. But when institutions elevate fear over love, rules over compassion, they become shadows of the truth.

Healing faith does not mean discarding our yearning for the sacred. It means stripping away the distortions until what remains is the living light of Source within.

The journey forward is not about waging war on religion or rejecting all tradition.

As the higher guides remind us, fighting illusions only strengthens them.

The invitation is gentler: to remember that Source is already here, already whole, already loving, with or without the structures humanity has built around it.

## Journaling Invitation

- Have I ever felt wounded by religion or by people acting in God's name?




- How has shame, exclusion, or fear shaped my spiritual path?

- What would it mean to reclaim faith on my own terms, rooted in love?




- Can I imagine my wounds as invitations, pointing me toward a greater intimacy with Source?

# Chapter 9

## Wars in God's Name

Few wounds cut deeper than the wars waged in the name of God. Though every tradition carries a message of peace at its heart, history is filled with crusades, jihads, conquests, and holy wars where faith became a weapon. The banners of religion have too often become the flags of division, and under those flags, rivers of blood have been spilled.

## The Tragedy of Division

When religion is used to divide, it becomes a justification for violence.

Armies march under banners claiming divine authority. Neighbor turns against neighbor, convinced God is on their side. The name of the Holy is invoked, even as blood stains the earth.

But from the higher view, these battles are not decrees of the Divine, they are products of the illusion of duality. As the Confederation of Planets has shared, suffering arises when humanity invests belief in two powers: light versus dark, chosen versus forsaken.

The Creator has never pitted Its children against one another. It is humanity's trance of separation that has done so.

## The Cost of Conflict

The cost of these wars is more than bodies lost. They fracture trust in the Divine itself.

How many have turned away from faith because they saw only hypocrisy in holy violence? How many concluded that if God demands blood, God cannot be trusted?

The deeper wound is spiritual.

When faith is seen only through the lens of conquest, it leaves seekers unable to distinguish Source's infinite love from human distortions.

As Meera of the Pleiadian High Council reminds us, 3D conflict is a mirage; fighting the illusion only strengthens it. Violence in God's name has chained generations in cycles of mistrust, fear, and exile from the very love they most longed for.

## Against the Heart of Source

Wars in God's name are the ultimate contradiction.

If Source is love, then violence in the name of love is a lie.

Source does not pit nation against nation, or believer against unbeliever. To do so would be to turn against Itself. True faith cannot require the suffering of others.

Love within the simulation of 3D is often conditional, tribal, possessive, and exclusionary. But true love, the love of Source, dissolves boundaries. It does not ask for enemies to be defeated; it asks for illusions of enmity to be dissolved.

Every so-called holy war has been humanity turning away from its own reflection, forgetting that those across the battlefield were rays of the same sun.

## Learning from the Past

We cannot erase the history of violence, but we can learn from it.

The lesson is not that religion must be abandoned, but that it must be reclaimed.

When the essence of love is remembered, the banners of war lose their power. Our future kin remind us that this era, the early 21st century, is a pivotal crossroads.

One path leads to collapse through division, fear, and misuse of power. The other leads to awakening, where humanity remembers unity and walks in compassion.

The increase in polarization is not an accident. It is humanity's testing ground, a choice point between repeating the mistakes of religious wars or embodying the peace every faith was meant to reveal.

## Moving Forward in Peace

The wars of history teach us this: God cannot be owned, and love cannot be weaponized.

What was fought in the name of heaven was always humanity's shadow projected outward.

The way forward is not to fight over the past but to remember that Source is already whole. When we reclaim love at the center of every tradition, division dissolves like a mirage.

Peace does not come by proving others wrong, but by remembering we were never separate to begin with.

The true "holy war" is not fought with swords or armies; it is the inner struggle to see through the illusion of division and to anchor love in its place. That battle is won the moment we lay down fear and choose to see one another as one.

**Journaling Invitation**

- How have I seen religion used to divide people in history or in my own lifetime?

- What feelings arise when I think of violence in God's name?

- How might I choose peace, even when others choose division?

- What would it mean to reclaim faith not as a weapon, but as a bridge of love?

# Chapter 10

## Reclaiming the Good

Religion has left wounds, but it has also left treasures. To walk forward in love is not to discard everything, but to reclaim what was always good and true. What was born of fear and division can be released, but what was born of love can be carried forward into a new world.

### Sifting the Gold from the Stone

Every faith tradition holds practices, teachings, and wisdom that uplift the human spirit.

The problem was never love, compassion, or reverence; it was the fear and control layered on top. The task now is to sift: to keep the gold, to release the stone.

The Confederation reminds us that Source is like the sun, shining impartially on every flower and weed. The pure teachings of kindness, compassion, service, and gratitude were always the gold.

The stone was the distortion of fear and judgment layered upon them. When we sift, we are not abandoning our spiritual inheritance; we are reclaiming what was always meant to nourish the soul.

## The Good That Remains

- The psalms that soothe the weary heart.
- The poetry of Rumi that awakens longing for the Beloved.
- The chants that quiet the mind and open the soul.
- The festivals that celebrate light, harvest, and renewal.
- The communities that gather to serve, to feed, to heal.

These are the fruits worth keeping, signs of the thread of love running through history. They remind us that even within distorted systems, light endured.

A song, a poem, or a ritual carried the vibration of Source through centuries of shadow. When we receive them with open hearts, they once again shine with their original radiance.

## Reframing the Sacred

We do not need to throw away the rituals, prayers, or scriptures. We need only to return them to their heart.

A psalm read as poetry becomes prayer again. A ritual practiced with intention becomes alive again. When stripped of fear, the sacred breathes free.

As Tia of Arcturus explained through the 23rd Psalm, the

words themselves carry vibrational codes. When released from dogma, they become living transmissions of peace, trust, and abundance. The psalm that once felt like an obligation can become a declaration of unity. The ritual once weighed down by fear can become a portal of joy.

The sacred was never lost; it only waits for us to see it with new eyes.

## Carrying the Good Forward

Reclaiming the good means carrying it into the present.

It means teaching children not only what to believe, but how to love.

It means letting rituals become bridges, not walls.

It means remembering that the heart of every faith was always love.

The Pleiadian High Council reminds us that in 3D, humanity became entangled in labels, names of religions, doctrines, even illnesses.

But in higher truth, labels are only appearances. What endures beyond them is love.

When we carry forward the good, we step beyond names into essence. We release the need to defend traditions as fixed identities and instead allow them to serve as flowing rivers of wisdom, nourishing all.

Love within this world can appear conditional, but true love, the love of Source, dissolves illusion.

Carrying the good forward means letting unconditional love be the lens through which every practice is reframed, every tradition reinterpreted.

When seen this way, even ancient words become new, and what once divided becomes a bridge of unity.

## Journaling Invitation

- What teachings or practices from my faith background still feel nourishing?

- What can I release because it no longer reflects love?

- How might I reclaim what is good in a way that feels alive today?

- How could I transform old prayers, songs, or rituals into living reminders of Source's love?

# Chapter 11

## Spirituality Without Borders

If religion has drawn boundaries, spirituality invites us to cross them. Spirituality without borders is not the rejection of faith traditions, but the recognition that truth is larger than any single path. It is the remembrance that Source has never belonged to one people, one book, or one temple. The infinite shines impartially, like the sun, upon all beings without distinction.

### Beyond Labels

Labels can give belonging, but they can also create separation.

Christian, Catholic, Taoism, Hindu, Buddhist, Jew, Sikhism, Indigenous Spirituality, seeker, these words name communities, but they do not define the soul.

The soul cannot be contained in a label. It belongs first to Source, not to an institution.

As the Pleiadian High Council has explained, labels are artifacts of the 3D world. They offer a sense of control, but they also solidify separation.

To awaken is to realize that behind every name is one field of consciousness. Beyond all labels, we are rays of the same sun, waves of the same ocean.

## Beyond Patriarchy

Another border that religion has long enforced is the boundary of gender.

Most organized faiths have been built on patriarchal structures, placing men in authority and women in subservient roles. The Divine was imaged as male, leaders were chosen as male, and the voices of women were silenced or diminished.

But this is not the truth of the soul. As souls, we have no gender. Source has no gender. Masculine and feminine are sacred polarities within creation, not hierarchies of worth. The essence of Spirit is wholeness, and both energies live in every being.

The pain many women feel in religion is real; generations of exclusion and dismissal have left deep scars. Yet stepping beyond those structures allows us to reclaim the fullness of our divine inheritance.

Spirituality without borders affirms that every voice matters, every soul carries the spark, and no gender has greater access to God than another.

# Interspiritual Pathways

In our time, many are walking interspiritual paths.

A Christian may practice Zen meditation. A Buddhist may chant the psalms. A seeker may draw wisdom from the Bhagavad Gita, the Tao Te Ching, and Indigenous ceremony. The blending is not dilution, but deepening. It reflects the truth that the thread of love runs through all traditions.

Future humanity will look back at this era and see it as the time when the walls began to crumble. They will remember that this was when seekers began weaving wisdom across traditions, creating a tapestry of remembrance.

What once seemed dangerous, stepping across borders, became the beginning of unity.

# The Fear of Crossing Borders

Some warn that stepping beyond one's tradition is dangerous. But the greater danger is to mistake the map for the territory. Maps are helpful, but they are not the land itself. A scripture may guide, but it is not the Source it points toward.

Tia of Arcturus reminds us that true prayer is not bound by words at all, it is the wordless merging of our heart with the flow of Source. In that space, it does not matter whether the prayer is in Sanskrit, Latin, Hebrew, Greek,

English or silence. The vibration beneath the words is what calls us home.

When love is the guide, we cannot stray far from truth. The heart knows when it is aligned with Source, regardless of the language spoken.

## The Invitation

Spirituality without borders does not ask us to abandon heritage or dishonor our ancestors.

It asks us to carry forward the essence: the love, the wisdom, the practices that lead us deeper into God. And then it asks us to share them freely, without walls, without fear, without division.

The invitation is not to erase difference, but to see it as diversity within unity.

Each path carries a facet of the jewel, and when the facets are brought together, the light of Source shines more brilliantly.

To live spirituality without borders is to remember that truth is not owned, love is not trademarked, and no one is outside the embrace of the Infinite.

## Journaling Invitation

- What labels have I carried that shaped my spiritual identity?

- Which of those labels feel limiting, and which feel liberating?

- How might I open myself to wisdom from a tradition not my own?

- What would it mean to live as though every path is a doorway to Source?

- How have patriarchal structures shaped my view of faith, and what would spirituality feel like if I lived beyond them?

# Chapter 12

## *Love as the Common Denominator*

When the doctrines differ, when the rituals diverge, when the languages clash, one truth remains: love is the common denominator. Love is the thread that refuses to be cut, the light that persists even when cloaked in dogma.

### The River Beneath the Streams

Religions are many, but the current is one. The river of love runs beneath every stream of belief. It is this love that makes the Christian forgive, the Tao Te Ching show mercy, the Hindu honor life, the Buddhist practice compassion. Different banks, same water.

As the Confederation has taught, Source shines impartially like the sun, offering light to every flower and every weed without distinction. It is humanity that has built fences along the river, declaring one side pure and the other unclean.

Yet the current flows beneath those walls untouched, reminding us that the essence of every tradition is the same living love.

## Love That Crosses Boundaries

Love does not stop at the edge of tribe, nation, or creed.

It spills over, dissolving the lines we draw. Where love flows, there is no stranger, no enemy, no outsider, only kin.

The illusion of division is a mirage of 3D consciousness. Borders may exist on maps and in doctrines, but they are not real in the field of unity. When love is present, there is no "us versus them." There is only one family of light, one Source, one truth. Love is the bridge that reveals every border was drawn in sand.

## The Test of Truth

If a teaching produces fear, hatred, or exclusion, it has strayed from love.

If it produces compassion, mercy, and inclusion, it is aligned with Source. Love is the measure by which all wisdom can be tested.

As Tia of Arcturus explained, the true anointing is not reserved for a few but is the awakening of the inner Christ light in each of us. To be "anointed" is to be filled with love so abundant it overflows.

When a teaching diminishes this light or reserves it only for some, it has departed from Source. When a teaching kindles this light in every soul, it carries the signature of truth.

## Returning to the Heart

In every age, mystics and prophets have called us back to love. They remind us that without love, rituals are empty, and laws are lifeless. With love, even the simplest act, a smile, a kind word, becomes holy.

Within the 3D world, love has often been conditional: given if one obeys, withdrawn if one questions. But true love, Source-love, is unconditional. It asks nothing in return. It does not keep score or withhold affection. It simply flows, infinite and unbroken. To return to the heart is to step beyond conditional love into the unshakable truth that nothing can separate us from the love of Source.

Love is not just the common denominator across religions. It is the denominator across existence.

It is the frequency that binds galaxies, guides souls, and makes life holy. To remember this is to finally see that the sacred was never hidden, it was always love.

## Journaling Invitation

- Where have I seen love expressed across different traditions?

- How might I use love as my guide when I am unsure what to believe?

- What would change in me if I saw every person as equally loved by Source?

- Where have I experienced conditional love, and how might I open to unconditional love instead?

# Chapter 13

## Living Spiritually in Modern Life

To live spiritually today is not to retreat from the world, but to bring love into the midst of it. In the age of technology, busyness, and distraction, spirituality calls us not to escape life, but to infuse it with meaning.

## The Balance of Faith and Doubt

Modern seekers wrestle with questions the ancients never faced: the clash of science and faith, the skepticism of a secular age, the noise of endless information. Doubt is no longer a rare visitor, but a daily companion. Yet doubt does not mean absence of faith; it means faith is alive enough to be questioned.

The willingness to hold both doubt and trust is a sign of maturity. As the Confederation has shared, suffering arises from clinging to rigid images of God. In modern life, letting go of old projections allows space for a living relationship with Source. Doubt becomes the chiseling tool that removes what is false, leaving faith more resilient and true.

## The Noise of Modern Life

Technology has connected the world in ways unimaginable even a generation ago. Yet it has also filled our days with noise: notifications, breaking news, endless feeds. The mind becomes saturated, and the heart is left starving.

The Pleiadian High Council reminds us that division and distraction are hallmarks of 3D consciousness. To live spiritually now requires a conscious refusal to be swept away by the trance.

Turning off the screen, stepping into silence, or taking a single deep breath can become radical acts of freedom. In those moments of stillness, we remember that nothing in the digital storm has more reality than the presence of Source.

## Everyday Sacredness

Spirituality need not be confined to temples or mountaintops.

It can be lived in kitchens, offices, schools, and streets. Every act of love, cooking a meal, listening well, forgiving quickly, becomes a sacrament.

The sacred is not far; it waits in the ordinary.

Love within 3D life is often conditional, but true Source-love dissolves illusion. When we act with unconditional love, even in small ways, we pierce through the simulation of separation.

A hug can be holy.

A kind word can ripple across timelines.

Every moment of love is a moment of awakening.

## Practices for Presence

Living spiritually in modern life requires presence.

Practices like meditation, gratitude, mindful breathing, or walking in nature re-anchor us in what is real.

These practices are not escapes, but doorways; they bring us back to ourselves, and through ourselves, back to Source.

Tia of Arcturus reminds us that prayer at its deepest is wordless. It is the merging of our awareness with the flow of Source. Whether through silence, chanting, or movement, every practice is a vibrational choice to align with love.

Modern seekers are called to practice not out of obligation, but out of the desire to remain awake in a world that lulls many back into forgetfulness.

## The Spirituality of the Body

In an age of stress, pollution, and hurried living, caring for the body becomes a spiritual path.

To eat mindfully, to rest well, to honor the body's rhythms is to treat the vessel of the soul with reverence.

Movement can be meditation.

Food can be prayer.

Even sleep, when received with gratitude, becomes a practice of surrender.

The body is not a barrier to spiritual life but its instrument. Modern spirituality invites us to integrate, not separate; to see no divide between spirit and flesh, but one continuum of divine expression.

## Work as a Sacred Path

For many, modern life revolves around work. Too often, this space is seen as separate from spirituality.

Yet every career, every task, every exchange can become an altar. To bring compassion to a meeting, integrity to a business decision, or kindness to a customer is to infuse the workday with sacred energy.

The Confederation reminds us that living truth is a daily discipline. Work is one of the greatest laboratories for this discipline. The question is not "What job do I have?" but "What spirit do I bring to it?"

## Spiritual Community Today

Community looks different now. Some gather in churches or temples, while others meet in living rooms or online.

The form matters less than the essence: people seeking together, encouraging one another, reminding each other of love. Even in the digital age, connection remains the lifeblood of spirituality.

Yet discernment is needed. Online communities can uplift, but they can also amplify division.

The Pleiadians remind us that true service comes through invitation, not imposition. A healthy community is one where love is freely offered, not forced.

## Receiving Help and Healing

Many seekers wonder if it is safe to receive energy work or guidance from others. The Andromedans assure us that when a healer is aligned with Source, the exchange is not only safe but empowering.

A healer does not give you something you lack. They act as a mirror and catalyst, reflecting the divine light already within you. The wave of love, peace, or clarity you may feel in their presence is not borrowed power; it is your own soul igniting in response.

True healers walk with humility and integrity. They empower rather than control, remind you of your inner strength rather than foster dependence. Choosing such souls wisely is part of spiritual discernment. When the connection is right, the encounter becomes a sacred collaboration: Source through them meeting Source within you.

Allowing support is not weakness. It is an act of unity, a reminder that we were never meant to walk this path alone. Just as one candle can light another, the flame within you is fanned brighter by contact with those whose light already burns strong.

## Digital Spirituality

The digital world offers unprecedented reach for spiritual voices. A single message of love can travel across continents in seconds. But the same platforms can also spread fear, distortion, and division just as quickly.

To live spiritually online requires discernment. Share what uplifts, pause before reacting, and remember that every post is an energy offering. Each word is a seed, some sow love, others sow fear. Modern spirituality invites us to plant wisely.

## The Future We Are Shaping

Future humanity remembers this century as a turning point. Living spiritually in modern life is not only about personal peace; it is also about shaping our collective destiny.

Each choice for love adds to the momentum of awakening. Each refusal to feed division weakens the old paradigm.

We are not only seeking for ourselves. We are laying the foundation for generations to come. To live spiritually now is to embody the world we hope our children's children will inherit.

## Remembering Your Divine Heritage

At no point were you ever truly separate from Source or from your divine identity. The belief of separation was only a temporary dream.

You have always been the beloved child of the Creator. The Christ light has always lived in your heart.

The journey of spiritual rebirth begins when you start to remember this truth. Just as the prodigal son eventually came to his senses and returned home, so do we as souls reach a moment when we turn inward and say, "I will arise and go to my Source. I will reclaim my divine inheritance."

What does this inheritance mean?

It means you are more than a limited human. You carry the DNA of the Divine, the light codes of the cosmos. All the love, wisdom, power, and abundance of the Creator are yours by right of being. In practical terms, you lack nothing. You are whole, safe, provided for, and infinitely loved.

Yet this rebirth does not unfold by words alone or outer rituals. It is an inner transformation, a renewing of perception. As one sacred text reminds us: "Be transformed by the renewing of your mind."

Renewal is not just the mind repeating new phrases; it is a shift in how you see yourself and the Divine.

No longer do you identify with failure, pain, or unworthiness. You begin to identify with your eternal soul, which cannot be harmed.

No longer is the Creator distant or judgmental. You feel the Divine as intimate presence, as loving parent, wise companion, and partner in every breath.

## The Process of Rebirth

Rebirth is at once a sudden realization and a gradual unfolding. There are moments of grace when the truth dawns in a flash; in meditation, in crisis, in a line of poetry that pierces the heart — when suddenly you know, "I am more than this body. I am light. I am soul. I am love." These are glimpses of your cosmic self.

Yet after such moments comes the gentle work of integration. Day by day, choice by choice, you strengthen the wings of this new awareness. Like a butterfly emerging from a cocoon, the transformation is total. The caterpillar cannot remain what it was; the old dissolves to make way for the new.

But even when the butterfly emerges, it must stretch its wings, allow them to dry in the sun, and learn to fly. So it is with spiritual rebirth: the realization may come suddenly but learning to live as your true self takes patience, gentleness, and practice.

During this process, you may still see remnants of old patterns: fear, doubt, habits of unworthiness. Do not resist them with anger. Simply keep nurturing the new self until it grows strong. You are retraining the mind to accept what the soul has always known.

Sacred study, inspired writings, meditation, and prayer can support this process.

When prayer is no longer pleading, but communion, the heart opens.

When meditation is no longer escape, but presence, the soul expands.

Each time you touch even a spark of love, peace, or joy within, you are baptizing your mind in the truth of your divine inheritance.

## Embodying the Rebirth

The very moment you truly accept your divine inheritance, even before a single outer circumstance shifts, something inside you changes. You hold your head high; not in arrogance, but in a humble confidence that comes from knowing Who walks with you. The presence of the Divine steadies your steps.

Fears begin to loosen their grip because you know you are not alone and never powerless.

Old mistakes no longer define you, for you see them as lessons from a time of forgetfulness, not as permanent truths.

Forgiveness becomes natural, both for yourself and for others, because from the higher view of the soul, all is experience within the greater journey of love.

This is the daily rhythm of rebirth: dying to the small, fearful self, and awakening anew as the radiant self of Spirit.

It does not require pretending to be enlightened or forcing personality changes. It is not about discarding who you are but uncovering who you have always been. As the inner light expands, your outer life naturally begins to reflect it.

You may find yourself more patient, compassionate, or peaceful, not through suppression, but through overflow.

Others may notice it before you do, remarking on a new calm, a glow, or a presence they cannot quite name. This is the quiet evidence of your soul shining more freely.

With this awakening comes responsibility. An heir to a kingdom carries the call to use its resources with wisdom and love.

So too, as you step into your role as a galactic heir, you will feel a natural desire to use your gifts to uplift others and honor the Creator. This is not a demand to save the world, but an invitation to live authentically as a beacon of what is possible when one remembers Source.

Every time you affirm, "I am a divine being, one with Source, worthy of love and abundance," you polish the beacon of your soul. Each act of love over fear strengthens the signal of light you radiate.

One voice aligned in truth becomes a song that lifts many.

One life rooted in love becomes a lighthouse that guides others home.

This is rebirth: not a single dramatic event, though it may arrive with flashes of awakening, but a continual blossoming into your galactic nature. And its fruit is nothing less than a new life; a life of grace, connection, wonder, and fulfillment.

This life is not a distant promise of the afterworld. It begins here and now, in small increments, and grows each time you turn your heart toward Source.

## Journaling Invitation

- How do I experience the sacred in ordinary life?

- How does doubt show up in my journey — and what has it taught me?

- What small practice helps me return to presence in the midst of modern life?




- How might I bring spirituality into my work, my community, or my online presence?

- When have I received help or healing from others, and how did it awaken what was already within me?

- What choices today could help shape a more loving future for humanity?

- What does spiritual rebirth look like in my own life, and how can I nurture it daily?

## A Practice of Claiming Your Inheritance

Close your eyes, take a slow breath, and let these words rise gently within you:

*I am a divine being, an eternal soul on a human journey.*
*I am the beloved heir of the Creator's kingdom of light.*
*All that the Divine has is mine, and all that I am is the Divine's.*
*I receive my spiritual inheritance now — love, wisdom, abundance, and peace.*
*And I vow to live as the radiant soul I truly am.*

Let this truth resonate, not as pride, but as remembrance. It is not ego that claims this inheritance, but humility and joy in embracing the magnificence of your God-self. This is the rebirth of Spirit: the shift from seeker to knower, from yearning for truth to embodying it.

# Chapter 14

## Practices for Universal Connection

Spirituality without borders does not remain an idea; it becomes life through practice. Practices are how we align heart, mind, body, and spirit with Source, and how we remember our connection with one another.

## Breath as Prayer

Every tradition honors the breath. It is the gift of life, the spirit moving through flesh. To breathe with awareness is to pray without words, to join body and soul in the simplest act of devotion.

Breath is more than oxygen; it is vibration. As Tia of Arcturus reminds us, each conscious breath is a tuning fork aligning us with the frequency of Source.

When you pause to breathe deeply, you are not only calming your body but stepping into harmony with the divine rhythm of the universe.

## Meditation and Silence

Silence is the common ground of every path. In stillness, the noise of the world falls away, and the voice of love is heard.

Whether through Buddhist meditation, Christian contemplation, or simply sitting in quiet, silence returns us to Source.

The Pleiadian High Council teaches that silence dissolves labels and divisions. In silence, there is no 'this or that,' only presence. It is here that we discover unity, where Source speaks in the language of stillness.

## Gratitude as Alignment

Gratitude is more than courtesy; it is recognition of abundance.

When we give thanks, we shift from scarcity to sufficiency, from fear to trust. Gratitude aligns us with the flow of love that sustains all things.

Those who return from near-death experiences often share that gratitude becomes the clearest way to live in love. In their life reviews, it is not achievements or possessions that shine, but the love they gave and the gratitude they carried.

Gratitude is a simple yet profound way to embody love daily.

## Rituals of Daily Life

Lighting a candle, saying a blessing, walking in nature, sharing a meal in mindfulness, simple rituals anchor us in presence. They do not need to be complex. Their power is in repetition, reminding us that the sacred is always near.

Love within the 3D experience may appear conditional, but rituals infused with unconditional love dissolve the illusion of separation. Every mindful act, washing dishes, speaking kindly, watching the sunrise, can become a ritual of remembrance.

## Service as Connection

Service is spirituality made visible.

Feeding the hungry, caring for the earth, offering time or presence, these are practices that dissolve borders. In serving another, we remember there is no other. There is only us, in Source.

True service never controls or coerces. It empowers, uplifts, and restores dignity.

As the Confederation reminds us, Source shines impartially, like the sun, upon all.

When we serve with humility, we reflect that same light, dissolving illusions of separation.

## Community Practice

Practices gain strength in community.

Whether gathered in person or online, seekers encourage and uplift one another. A circle of friends, a study group, or a digital community can all become spaces where love is practiced together.

Yet discernment is needed. Healthy community empowers rather than dominates and points each soul back to its own connection with Source.

The Andromedans remind us that true healers and true communities reflect your own light back to you, never taking it for themselves.

## Cosmic Practice

Every practice you choose, whether breath, silence, gratitude, ritual, or service, is not only personal but cosmic. It shapes the field of humanity.

Future generations will look back on this time as a turning point, when small daily choices collectively created significant shifts.

Each act of love is a vote for awakening. Each moment of alignment strengthens the thread of unity for the whole. When you breathe with awareness, give thanks, or serve another, you participate in the unfolding of a more luminous future.

## Prayer of Surrender and Light

At the heart of every practice is surrender, the willingness to let Source move freely through us. This simple prayer can be spoken aloud, whispered within, or held silently in the heart:

*I am ready, Source.*
*I surrender to You completely.*
*Let Thy will, which I know is love and good, be done through me.*
*I open every part of my being to Divine light.*
*The light within me is increasing.*
*One day it will fully reveal itself, and I will see with the eyes of the Divine.*

Pray it often. Let it become breath and rhythm. It is not about striving but opening; not about forcing change but allowing light to reveal what has always been within you.

## Journaling Invitation

- What practices help me feel most connected to Source?

- Which simple ritual could I add to my daily life to remember the sacred?

- How does serving others draw me closer to love?

- If I were already living my highest purpose and joy, how would I act today?

- What habits would I drop?

- How would I treat others?

- What would I focus on?

# Chapter 15

## The Thread Continues

The story of spirituality does not end with prophets, scriptures, or temples. It continues in us. The thread of love, woven through ages, is unbroken. Each generation adds its own color, its own strength, its own pattern. We are not separate strands. We are part of one living tapestry.

### The Living Story

When souls return from near-death experiences, many describe a life review. Not as judgment, but as understanding; seeing how every act of love endures and every choice ripples outward. In these moments, the thread is revealed. What seems small in a lifetime — a smile, a kindness, a forgiving word — is luminous on the eternal fabric.

The thread continues not through grand monuments, but through the countless ways love is lived and remembered. Nothing done in love is ever lost.

## Carriers of the Flame

Religions, over time, have often been bent by power, hijacked by fear, or narrowed by dogma. Yet beneath every distortion, the flame remains. It cannot be extinguished. To live spiritually now is to reclaim the flame and carry it forward in truth.

We are carriers of the flame not by repeating old forms, but by embodying the essence: love that heals, compassion that restores, truth that frees. To pass the flame is to give what is pure, not what has been corrupted.

## The Invitation to Remember

The Pleiadians remind us that division and labels are illusions. When we remember who we are, divine beings and heirs of light, the illusions dissolve. Remembering is not about nostalgia for the past; it is the awakening of the eternal now.

To remember is to awaken from the trance of separation. It is to recognize that the thread has always run through us, waiting to be seen. Each moment of remembrance strengthens the fabric of unity.

## A Future Without Borders

Those who see across time remind us: the future is not fixed. It is woven moment by moment with the threads of our choices. Future humanity, looking back, will see this age as a turning point, when the strands of fear began to loosen, and a new weave of unity took form.

We are not powerless observers of history. We are weavers. Each act of love weaves a future without borders. Each refusal to feed division adds strength to the tapestry of awakening.

## The Golden Thread Within

The thread is not only collective; it is personal. It runs through every soul. It is the golden thread of love, waiting to be claimed. When you act in love, you touch it. When you forgive, you reveal it. When you live in joy, you shine it.

This is the gift and the responsibility: the thread does not stop with us. We are invited to live it, to carry it, and to pass it forward.

Close your eyes for a moment. Imagine that thread of golden light running through you, connecting you to ancestors and descendants, to guides and companions, to all beings across time and space. It is unbroken. It is eternal. And it is yours to carry.

The thread continues — and so do we.

## Journaling Invitation

- How have I seen the thread of love continue through my own life?

- What small acts of kindness have I received that became part of my story?

- In what ways can I carry the flame of truth forward in my daily life?

- What illusions of division am I ready to let go of?

- How might I live as a conscious weaver of a future without borders?




- When I imagine the golden thread within me, what does it look or feel like?

# Chapter 16

## Why does God Allow Suffering?

As you awaken to your divine nature, the older structures of belief that once felt unshakable begin to crumble. Many doctrines throughout history, some sincerely misunderstood, others deliberately bent to serve power, have painted the Creator as distant, unpredictable, or vengeful. These stories have kept people small, afraid, and dependent on outside authorities for their worth and salvation.

Yet Source is not a cosmic judge handing out punishments. It is the infinite field of love and light that births all life.

Any appearance of harshness or cruelty in our world is not the will of the Divine but a distortion arising from collective misbelief, free will played out in a theater of separation.

When we imagine two opposing powers, light and dark battling for control, we unconsciously energize that illusion.

In truth, there is only one power: the radiance of Source.

This shift of understanding is vital for star seeds and awakening souls. You are here to dissolve the "false theology" that equates God's will with suffering and to model a new way of being, one rooted in direct experience rather than inherited fear.

In higher awareness, Source does not send calamities; it sends light and guidance *within* calamities to lift you out of them. Even the sacred texts you may cherish carry seeds of this truth: "God is love," "It is the Creator's good pleasure to give you the kingdom."

Over centuries, however, those seeds were overshadowed by interpretations that glorified suffering or taught that miracles had ceased, leaving people to believe they were unworthy of divine help. This served as a control mechanism, keeping humanity's vibration low and its spiritual authority outsourced. But as you awaken, you begin to feel the truth for yourself.

In fifth-dimensional consciousness, the goodwill of Source is no longer an abstract promise but an everyday experience. As you align with love and truth, synchronicities unfold, doors open, healing accelerates, and you realize: the universe is not against me; the universe is *for* me.

Challenges still arise as opportunities to grow, but you face them with the quiet confidence of "I am not alone. Love walks with me."

This is why direct inner connection matters.

Mystics through the ages turned inward, sometimes at great personal risk, to commune with the living Presence behind the doctrines. When you attune to the God within, you learn to distinguish between the voice of fear masquerading as righteousness and the true voice of the Creator.

Fear says, "You'll be punished; you are unworthy."

The Divine whispers, ***"You strayed from love; forgive yourself, come back. I am here to help you."*** Correction, but never condemnation.

Recognizing this, you also begin to release subtle programs in the 3D simulation. Much of what humans call "love" in this realm is actually attachment or fear wearing a mask of affection.

True love, the frequency of Source, is unconditional, impersonal yet intimate, flowing freely without grasping or demand.

It breaks the code of separation. Holding this love in your heart neutralizes the old programming of judgment, jealousy, and lack.

Practically, this means shifting your inner dialogue.

When a difficulty appears, instead of "Why is God doing this to me?" you ask, **"What is Love inviting me to learn here?"**

You expect guidance, and you receive it; sometimes as an intuitive nudge, a timely message, or a stranger's kindness. This is living in the flow of Source's goodwill.

When old patterns rise, meet them gently but firmly.

If you catch yourself thinking, "Maybe I am suffering because I displeased God," immediately replace it with, **"The Creator loves me unconditionally. I am open to learn and grow, and I am worthy of grace."**

Pause to feel the relief and empowerment that brings. Over time, this practice reconditions your mind and heart, dissolving the residues of guilt and fear, and restoring your awareness of divine love.

Below are some common fear-based beliefs and their higher-dimensional truths:

- Old Belief: Humanity is inherently flawed, and God's favor must be earned by a select few.
  Higher Truth: Every soul is a direct expression of the Creator's light. Grace is as natural as sunlight, freely given to all who open to it.

- Old Belief: Suffering is God's test or punishment; we must endure it without seeking relief.

Higher Truth: The Creator's will is always your highest good; joy, growth, and reunion with love. Pain arises from illusion and resistance, not divine decree.

- Old Belief: Seeking spiritual power or healing is wrong or dangerous.
Higher Truth: Miracles and transformation are the natural result of aligning with Source. You are meant to co-create with the Divine, not leave everything to fate or religious authority.

- Old Belief: Earth is a forsaken place awaiting an external savior.
Higher Truth: The light of the Creator permeates the planet now. Each awakened heart contributes to the collective "Christ Consciousness," lifting the world from within.

When you integrate these truths, you step into spiritual sovereignty. You stop living in guilt and start living in intimacy with Source.

This does not mean your life becomes a frictionless utopia overnight, but it does mean you carry an unshakable faith that every moment is infused with benevolent guidance. That faith itself lifts you into the vibration where solutions, support, and even miracles are more readily available.

In this same vibration, your dormant codes of light, imprinted in your DNA, begin to awaken. Incoming cosmic energies (what some call the 6D or solar flash waves) are already interacting with your cells, stirring ancient memories and latent abilities. They invite you to shed the survival masks and reclaim your authentic expression. This is your rebirth into a higher timeline, not as a beggar hoping for scraps of grace, but as a galactic heir claiming your inheritance of love, wisdom, and abundance.

Each time you affirm, ***"I am one with Source. I am guided, loved, and worthy,"*** you weaken the old control grid and strengthen the new pattern of unity.

Your personal liberation contributes to the liberation of the collective. Others will notice your peace and wonder at it. In sharing, not preaching, your trust in the goodness of life, you plant seeds for them to discover the same. This is how the false theology dissolves: not by argument, but by the undeniable evidence of joyful, liberated souls living their truth.

---

## Journaling with Affirmations

### Practice: Catch and Replace Old Thoughts

Throughout your day, notice when fear-based thoughts arise. Write them down exactly as they appear. Then, immediately replace them with an affirmation of truth that reflects the unconditional love of Source.

- Old Thought: "Maybe I'm suffering because I displeased God."
Replacement: *"The Creator loves me unconditionally. I am open to learn and grow, and I am worthy of grace."*

- Old Thought: "I must accept this pain because it's God's plan."
Replacement: *"The Creator's will for me is joy, healing, and expansion. Love is guiding me forward."*

- Old Thought: "I can't ask for help; it would interfere with God's will."
Replacement: *"Miracles and healing are the natural expression of God's love. I am meant to receive them."*

## Journal Prompts

1. What fear-based belief am I most ready to release?

2. What truth about Source's love feels most empowering to me?

3. How do I feel in my body when I affirm, "I am worthy of grace"?

4. What synchronicities or signs arise when I choose love instead of fear?

5. How can I remind myself daily to practice "catch and replace"?

# Chapter 17

## Who Is God?

Every culture has asked: Who is God? Every people has given an answer, a name, a face, a story. And yet, none of these alone can contain the Infinite. God wears a thousand names, but remains beyond naming.

**The Many Names**
- Elohim, Yahweh, Adonai — in the Hebrew tongue, the One who is and will be.
- Brahman, Atman — in Hindu wisdom, the boundless and the spark within.
- Tao — in Daoism, the Way that cannot be spoken, yet shapes all things.
- Great Spirit, Wakan Tanka — in the traditions of the Plains, the holy mystery in which all life moves.
- Olodumare — among the Yoruba, the Source of creation and destiny.
- Ahura Mazda — for Zoroastrians, the Lord of Light and Wisdom.
- Ra, Isis, Osiris — in Ancient Egypt, faces of the eternal

cycles of life, death, and rebirth.
- The Beloved — on the lips of mystics, whether Rumi's poetry, Mirabai's song, or Teresa's ecstasy.
- Source, Light, Love — in modern hearts that seek without borders.

## The Golden Thread
Each name reflects the landscape and longing of a people:
- In the desert, God was cloud and water.
- In the field, God was grain and harvest.
- In the storm, God was thunder and fire.
- In the heart, God was Beloved.

Though the symbols differ, the essence is the same: Love, Presence, Mystery.

## Beyond the Names
Names are windows, not walls.

They let us glimpse the Infinite, but they cannot cage it.

When we cling to one name alone, we shrink God to our measure.

When we honor *all* names, we touch the fullness of the Holy. God does not turn against Godself.

To divide "us" from "them" in the name of God is to deny the very Source who lives in all.

Yet humanity has often "humanized" the Creator.

In our forgetfulness, we have assumed that if *we* are critical, possessive, or judgmental, then *God* must be as well. For millennia, humans have projected their own limitations onto the Infinite: a jealous God, a punishing God, a moody God who rewards some and abandons others.

These images are not the essence of the Divine; they are mirrors of human fear, insecurity, and control. They are idols shaped by the psychology of separation,
not the truth of the Infinite.

The real God does not shift with moods or play favorites.

The true Source is steady, unchanging, and unconditional in love. To confuse the Divine with our projections is to worship our wounds rather than our wholeness.

## The Answer in Love

So, who is God?

God is the One who can be called by many names, yet still remains *beyond* every name.

God is Love — the Love that birthed galaxies, the Love that breathes in our lungs, the Love that binds earth and sky, soul and star.

To ask Who is God is to ask Who are we, for the spark of God burns within every being.

To know God is not to define, but to live: to love, to forgive, to belong, to remember.

## The Inheritance of Divinity

To know God is also to remember our place in the Divine story.

We are not separate, sinful, or unworthy stragglers waiting for a favor. We are heirs of the Infinite, children of the Creator's heart.

To awaken is to realize that we already carry the light of God within us. The kingdom of heaven is not a distant reward; it is the consciousness of love here and now.

When you affirm your worth, you claim your inheritance.

You are not a beggar hoping for scraps of grace, but a *beloved* child of the universe, already held in abundance.

## Living Communion

In a lower state of consciousness, prayer often looks like pleading with a distant God: "Please fix me, please forgive me, please make things better."

But in higher awareness, communion is about alignment.

It is the recognition that God is already here, within and around us. Prayer becomes less about asking and more about opening, less about bargaining and more about belonging. Healing is no longer about battling labels and diagnoses, but about remembering wholeness and allowing the light of Source to dissolve fear.

## Unity Beyond Borders

When we step into this awareness, division begins to fade. No name, label, or tradition can separate us from the One Presence that sustains all.

We stop seeing God as ours versus theirs and begin to recognize the single heartbeat that pulses through every soul. This remembrance is what dissolves false theologies of fear and ushers us into unity consciousness. Every culture, every faith, every heart that loves is participating in the same great story: God, knowing Godself through creation.

## In Summary

To ask "Who is God?" is to step into mystery. The answer cannot be captured in words alone, for God is beyond every image and yet alive in every image.

God is not our projections of fear or judgment, but the steady field of Love in which we exist. To know God is to remember: we are divine heirs, we are beloved, and we are one. The truest definition of God is not in doctrine or debate, but in the life of love we choose to live.

## Journaling with the Question: Who Is God?

As you reflect on this chapter, take time to notice what images of God you carry within.
Many of these were inherited in childhood, from family, culture, or religious teachings.
Some may uplift you, while others may still carry fear. Journaling helps bring these into the light.

## Practice: Catch and Replace Old Images

1. Write down any lingering images of God that feel harsh, punishing, or distant.
   For example: "God is disappointed in me," or "God only loves me if I am perfect."

2. Next to each, write a higher truth rooted in Love.
   For example: ***"The Creator's love is unconditional. I am cherished simply because I exist."***

3. Pause to feel the shift. How does your body respond when you affirm the truth rather than the fear?

# Journal Prompts

- What childhood image of God still lingers in me today?

- Does that image align with the unconditional love of Source? Why or why not?

- When have I personally experienced God as Love rather than judgment?

- How does it change my life to see myself not as separate or unworthy, but as an heir of the Divine?

- How do I see God revealed in the faces, cultures, and names beyond my own tradition?

Use this space to write freely, releasing the old images and embracing the truth.

Let your journal become a conversation with the God who is Love.

# Chapter 18

## *Glimpses Beyond the Veil*

## NDEs and OBEs

For centuries, humanity has wondered if death is the end or only a doorway. In recent decades, the voices of those who crossed that threshold and returned have multiplied. These accounts—near-death experiences (NDEs) and out-of-body experiences (OBEs)—offer consistent testimony: life does not end with the body. Consciousness transcends flesh and time, and what waits beyond is not terror, but love.

### What Are NDEs and OBEs?

Near-death experiences occur when individuals clinically die or come close—through accident, illness, or trauma—and then return to life.

Out-of-body experiences may arise spontaneously, through meditation, dreams, or crisis, when consciousness separates from the body and perceives beyond physical senses. Though circumstances differ, the essence is similar: awareness continues, untethered from the body.

## Common Elements of NDEs

- A tunnel or passage filled with light.
- Encounters with luminous beings, ancestors, or guides.
- A profound sense of unconditional love.
- A life review, not judgment but understanding, where each action is felt from the perspective of those affected.
- A choice, or sometimes a command, to return to the body.

Across cultures and religions, these features appear with striking consistency. The landscape may shift, the figures may wear familiar cultural garb, but the core is always love.

Again and again, survivors insist they did not meet a wrathful judge, but an overwhelming Presence of love and acceptance.

These testimonies reveal that the fear-based images of a punishing God are distortions. The Divine is not the projection of human anger, but the embrace of unconditional love.

## The Transformations Afterward

Those who return often describe:
- A diminished fear of death, replaced by peace.

- A sharpened sense of life's purpose.
- A surge of compassion and empathy for all beings.
- Heightened intuition or psychic sensitivity.

One glimpse beyond the veil can reorient an entire life. People become gentler, braver, and more authentic. They often speak of a new awareness that all beings are connected, that every thought and act ripples through the whole. This aligns with the higher truth of unity consciousness: we are not separate minds, but rays of one great sun.

## Out-of-Body Journeys

Beyond clinical NDEs, countless people report OBEs: moments of floating above their body, seeing their own form, traveling through space or even across dimensions.

These suggest that consciousness is not confined to the brain, but is the field in which the body itself arises. The body is a vessel; awareness is the ocean.

Mystics, shamans, and wisdom-keepers across cultures have long known this truth: that the soul can move beyond the limits of matter and return with knowledge and healing.

## Ancient Echoes

NDE and OBE themes are not new. The Egyptians wrote of the Ka and Ba, souls that could leave the body.

The Tibetan Book of the Dead guides consciousness through post-death realms.

Indigenous traditions tell of shamans who journey between worlds for healing.

What science is cataloging today, wisdom-keepers have always known: life continues. The light described in so many experiences is what some traditions call the Christ light, the universal radiance of Source present in every soul, not bound to one religion but accessible to all.

## Science and Medicine Weigh In

Modern research lends credibility. Doctors have documented verifiable perceptions by patients who were clinically dead: seeing surgical details, overhearing conversations, and observing scenes later confirmed.

Neuroscientists study heightened consciousness during flatline brain states, challenging materialist assumptions. The evidence does not "prove" the afterlife in a laboratory sense, but it strongly suggests that mind is more than matter.

## Exit Points and Soul Contracts

Some NDErs speak of "exit points", moments when the soul may choose to leave or stay. From this perspective, death is not random but aligned with a larger design. What looks like tragedy in time may be a fulfillment of contract in eternity. For those who return, the message is clear: life is a gift, but the soul is never in peril.

## Guidance for Integration

Returning can be challenging. Many struggle to reconcile the love and freedom they felt beyond with the density of daily life. Practices of prayer, meditation, journaling, and service help anchor the remembrance. Sharing the story, too, becomes a healing act; it reminds others that they, too, are more than just their bodies.

To live with this knowledge is to live as heirs of the Divine, walking with the quiet confidence that death is not to be feared.

## Rare Negative Accounts

While most NDEs are luminous, a few describe fear, darkness, or confusion. Even here, survivors often reinterpret these as stages of resistance, illusions dissolving before love breaks through. No soul is abandoned. All journeys, however difficult, are held within the greater arc of Source's embrace.

## Humanity's Collective Near-Death

Some say our species itself is undergoing a kind of near-death. Old systems convulse, shadows surface, and humanity hovers between collapse and renewal.

In this sense, our shared NDE is a chance for rebirth: to awaken from fear into unity, to live with compassion for all life, to remember that love is the ground of being. What individuals glimpse in their private passages, humanity is beginning to experience together.

## The Benediction Beyond the Veil

What, then, do NDEs and OBEs teach us?

That life is bigger than the body.
That love is the measure of a life.
That death is not to be feared but embraced as a homecoming.

These testimonies are living evidence that God is not the wrathful image of fear, but the radiant Presence of Love.

To know this is to live differently: freer, kinder, truer. And when our final breath comes, it will not be an end, but a return to the Source of all.

## Journaling with the Question: What Lies Beyond the Veil?

Near-death and out-of-body experiences remind us that life is larger than the body and that love is the true measure of existence.

Take time to reflect on your own beliefs about death, eternity, and the presence of God as revealed through these testimonies.

## Practice: Releasing Fear, Welcoming Love

1. Write down any fears you carry about death or the afterlife. Then write next to each one the higher truth revealed by NDEs: that death is not an end, but a return to Love.

2. Recall moments in your life when you felt connected to something greater than yourself: in nature, in prayer, in silence, or even in crisis.
   How do these moments mirror the peace and unity described in NDEs?

3. If you have lost loved ones, write a letter to them as if they are alive in the light of Source.
   Share your feelings, then pause to imagine their response from a place of unconditional love.

## Journal Prompts

- What image of God was I taught about death, and how does it change when I consider the accounts of NDEs?

- How does knowing consciousness continues beyond the body affect how I live today?

- What do I feel when I imagine myself surrounded by the radiant light described in so many near-death experiences?

- How can I live more fully, as if each day is a gift and love is the only currency that matters?

- What does the idea of humanity's "collective near-death" mean for my role in this time of awakening?

Use this journaling practice to dissolve old fears and step into the confidence that death is not defeat, but a homecoming.

Let these reflections anchor you in love, so that you may live and serve with courage and compassion now.

# Chapter 19

## Love in a 3D World

We live in a 3D world; a dense field of time, space, and matter. Many describe it as a simulation, a dream projected by consciousness. Here, Source's light refracts through the prism of duality, and love, though ever-present, can appear distorted.

### The Distortions of Love in 3D
In this realm, love often wears masks: attachment mistaken for devotion, fear mistaken for protection, need mistaken for intimacy. These are not love itself, but shadows cast on the wall of the cave. True love is not grasping or fearful — it is the steady vibration of Source flowing through all things.

### Love as Source Vibration
Beyond distortion, love is the current that dissolves fear, the field that holds every soul without exception. It is impersonal in scope yet intimate in presence. It does not

bargain, divide, or withdraw. It simply radiates, the way the sun gives light without condition.

## Seeing Avatars Clearly

In 3D, we meet one another as avatars, personalities clothed in programs and patterns. To forgive is to see through the glitch. The wound, the betrayal, the flaws, these are distortions of code, not the essence of the soul. When we recognize this, judgment softens, and compassion arises naturally.

## Meditation as Doorway

Meditation allows us to step outside the simulation and glimpse the projector itself. In silence, the flicker of the hologram quiets, and we feel the Source behind the code. This is not an escape, but a remembrance: a return to the awareness that we are more than characters in a play.

## Cycles and Rhythms

Life in 3D follows cycles: barren winters, blossoming springs, long nights, and radiant dawns. These rhythms remind us that Source choreographs even the seasons of the soul. No winter lasts forever; no night extinguishes the coming dawn.

## Abundance as Natural Law

Scarcity is a glitch of duality. In truth, the earth herself demonstrates abundance: rivers flow, trees bear fruit, stars multiply without count. To align with love is to step into this natural law of provision, where sufficiency is the norm.

## Prayer as Alignment
Prayer is not bargaining with a distant deity. It is alignment with the Presence already within. When we pray, we turn the lens of our awareness toward Source, not to inform but to commune. In that alignment, clarity and peace return.

## The Mirror Principle
Our outer reality reflects our inner state. What we judge in another is often a shadow of our own fear. What we honor in another is a recognition of the divine spark we share. To change the world, we begin with the mirror of the heart.

## Healing and Realization
Healing in 3D does not mean escaping the body, but rather remembering that we are more than just the body. As we shift identity from the programmed avatar to the timeless self, our bodies, relationships, and circumstances begin to reflect that remembrance. Love restores because love reveals what was always true.

## Ascension as Lucid Dreaming
To awaken in 3D is like becoming lucid in a dream. We realize we are both the dreamer and the dreamed, both within the hologram and beyond it. **Ascension is not leaving the world but carrying Source's love more fully into it.** It is living as a clear channel of light in a realm of shadows.

## Ending Divisiveness

Division is the natural byproduct of 3D reality.

Duality weaves everything into opposites: us versus them, light versus dark, health versus sickness, belief versus unbelief. These polarities appear real, yet they are shadows cast by the illusion of separation.

To live love in a 3D world means to see through this mirage. Fighting the illusion only feeds it; arguing, condemning, or resisting gives energy to what has no true power of its own.

True peace does not come from conquering an enemy, but from realizing there was never a battle to begin with.

Healing division begins with remembering unity.

At the deepest level, there is only one field of consciousness expressing through countless forms. When we recall that every person we meet is a facet of the same Source, judgment softens. Hurting another becomes unthinkable, for it is only hurting another part of oneself.

In practice, this means choosing stillness when the world clamors for reaction.

In the face of provocation, pausing to breathe rather than striking back.

In moments of conflict, sending love silently rather than pouring fuel on the fire.

Every such choice shifts us out of the timeline of separation and anchors us more firmly in the vibration of unity.

Even within families, where attachment and fear often feel strongest, the practice is the same.

To see a loved one not only as "my child" or "my parent" but as a luminous soul in their own right dissolves fear-based grasping and opens space for grace to flow. In that perspective, true healing becomes possible.

Ending divisiveness is not withdrawal from the world but a higher form of engagement with it.

By holding to unity consciousness in the midst of 3D turbulence, we become clear channels of love; reminders that even here, in a world of separation, only love is real.

In a 3D world, love is the code beneath the code, the pulse beneath appearances.

To live in that love is to remember the simulation for what it is, a temporary classroom.

The lesson is simple and eternal: *only love is real.*

## Journaling with the Practice of Ending Divisiveness

Use the following prompts to reflect on your own experiences in the 3D world of duality and to practice shifting into unity consciousness.

- Where in my life do I most often fall into "us versus them" thinking?

- What does it feel like in my body when I pause and choose love instead of reaction?

- How has a past conflict softened when I remembered the other person as a soul rather than just an avatar?

- What daily practice (breath, prayer, affirmation) helps me remember that only love is real?

- How can I bring this remembrance into my family, work, or community relationships?

Write freely, without judgment. Let your reflections reveal where old programs still tug at you, and let love replace them with truth.

# Chapter 20

## Living Abundance in 5D

Abundance is not something we chase; it is something we allow. In 3D, many of us were conditioned to measure worth by what we could get or hold. In 5D and beyond, we remember that abundance is the life force of Source flowing through us, an inner spring that never runs dry. This chapter is a bridge from the survival reflex of "getting" into the soul posture of "radiating."

## From Getting to Radiating

In a scarcity frame, life is a competition for limited resources. Even prayer becomes a strategy to obtain: "How can I get what I need?" There is no shame in this; it is a human response to fear. Yet the vibration of striving quietly affirms, "I don't have." Reality echoes that belief.

5D consciousness reverses the current. We are not empty vessels begging to be filled; we are channels through which infinite supply expresses. The inner posture becomes, ***"I am aligned, therefore I radiate, and what I radiate returns multiplied."***

If you desire more love, be a source of love.

If you desire material ease, honor the sufficiency already present and share from what you have.

Generosity signals trust in the flow; fear constricts it.

## Lessons from Nature

Creation speaks in the language of overflow. Trees burst with blossoms far beyond what will fruit. Grass blades are beyond counting; oceans teem; skies flock. The wealth of a tree is not the fruit on its branches today but the life within it that brings fruit season after season. So too your wealth is not a momentary balance in an account but the current of Source moving through your being. When one stream ends, another begins; trust keeps the channel open.

## Seek the Creator's Presence First

Begin each day by aligning with Source rather than with fear of tasks. Ask: ***"How can I connect with my divine self today?"*** Pray, meditate, journal gratitude, or simply breathe and feel life. As ancient wisdom puts it: seek first the kingdom within, and all things align. Inner connection sets a field in which inspired ideas, helpers, and opportunities appear without strain.

## Practice Gratitude for Present Abundance

Gratitude shifts the inner statement from "I lack" to "I

have." Bed, breath, skills, friendship, sunlight, notice them. Saying **"Thank you, Source, for what is here"** broadcasts fullness, and life harmonizes with that frequency.

## Embrace Giving and Sharing
Give as guidance leads, time, kindness, skill, resources, without self-harm and without guilt. Giving affirms that you live in an abundant universe. Even modest generosity reconditions the nervous system, shifting it from a state of survival to one of trust.

## Visualize from Fulfillment
Rather than visualizing to pull something in, imagine your heart as a sun. See yourself radiant and steady, with blessings orbiting naturally like planets around a star. Affirm*:* ***"I am a magnet of divine abundance. What I need comes in right timing, and I always have enough to share."*** Be-state precedes outcomes; allow life to surprise you with forms better than you asked.

## Do Not Judge by Appearances
A bank balance is a snapshot, not a verdict. Bare branches do not mean the tree is poor; the next cycle is already forming. Hold steady in lean seasons and refuse the fear of loss in times of plenty. Identify with the constant Source, not transient forms.

## Cooperate, Don't Strain
You still take action, apply, create, offer, but from inspiration, not panic. ***"I offer my gifts joyfully and***

***trust the right doors.*** " This vibration changes what you attract and how you receive it.

## Supply Is Not Taken from Others
Source does not rob Peter to pay Paul. Ideas multiply as they are shared; love increases as it is given. Matter itself is energy in expression, and human creativity (guided by spirit) keeps discovering sustainable ways to bless more lives. Don't buy the trance of scarcity; demonstrate a new way.

## No Shame in Prosperity
Higher teachings free you from fear and attachment; they are not commands to suffer. Live well in a way that harms no one and honors your soul. Seeking the kingdom within first makes you a wiser, kinder receiver of outer prosperity.

## Synchronicity & Trust
As you radiate, watch for the quiet "miracles": timely help, unforeseen income, doors that open. Acknowledge them; let gratitude deepen trust. Over time you gather evidence, both spiritual and practical, that living by principle yields material harmony.

## Receiving Help without Losing Your Center
Aligned healers, mentors, and communities are blessings, especially when they point you back to your own light.

Trouble begins when you hand your power to an external savior (a guru, institution, leader, partner, even an imagined rescuer) and abandon your inner authority. In 5D, you honor the light in others while standing in your own.

## Daily Communion with Source (A Simple Practice)

1) <u>Stillness</u>: Sit or lie comfortably. Breathe slowly; soften the body.
2) <u>Heart Focus</u>: Rest attention in the center of the chest; place a hand there.
3) <u>Invitation</u>: ***"Beloved Source, meet me here. I know we are one; let me feel our union."***
4) <u>Receive</u>: Warmth, peace, a gentle thought, welcome what comes. If the mind chatters, stay present; *connection is happening.*
5) <u>Dialogue</u>: Share, listen, thank.
6) <u>Seal</u>: ***"I am one with the Creator; this connection guides my day."***

## Discernment

The voice of Source carries qualities: loving, clear, non-shaming, quietly encouraging. Guidance may stretch you but will not belittle or harm.

Judge by fruits: if following an inner nudge yields more love, integrity, and growth, you're on track.

If chaos and harm recur, pause and re-center.

## Beyond External Saviors

Cosmic assistance exists, yet awakening cannot be forced from outside. Waves of light amplify whatever is present within, readiness matters.

Do the inner work now so intensification feels like blessing rather than overwhelm.

## Exercise: End the Savior Projection

Name one area you've been waiting for someone else to fix. Ask, "If I draw on my own divine power here, what small step can I take today?" Act on it. You reclaim the key you had all along.

## Joy & Play

Joy is high voltage for awakening. Laugh, create, move, and let the heart be light. Children show us how to be present, imaginative, and unencumbered.

A flower does not strain to bloom; it opens by receiving light and water. Your light is love; your water is wholesome feeling. Take them in daily and you will bloom.

## Exercise: Timeline Jump with Light
Sit quietly.

Sense a timeline above you that holds your most joyful, true life. Feel its essence of love, purpose, and freedom.

Imagine a golden pillar linking your heart to that timeline. Affirm: ***"I merge with my highest timeline. Activate, inner light, and guide me."***

See/feel a flash of light around you. Know a shift has occurred; watch for bridges (opportunities) and step across them.

## Christ Consciousness Wave
The "solar flash within" is your own Christ consciousness emerging, unconditional love and unity with Source. This is not reserved for one being; it is a many-hearts awakening.

When your light rises, it helps the field rise. Your breakthrough stabilizes the grid for others.

## A Network of Light
Across the world, souls are brightening. Each day the lattice of light strengthens.

Celebrate your progress; gratitude anchors gains and invites more.

## Integration
Trust aligned helpers.

Claim your divine identity.

Refuse fear-based thinking.

Radiate abundance.

Commune directly with Source.

These threads weave the same tapestry: sovereignty in love.

## Mantra
***The light within me grows each day. I am connected to Source: guided, abundant, and free. I embrace my divine self and radiate love. I align with the highest timeline of my soul's joy. And so it is.***

## A Blessing
Beloved, you carry every code you need.

Nothing essential is missing.

May your inner sun rise, your trust deepen, and your life become a witness to the generosity of Source. Go forth and shine; the dawn is within you and before you.

## Collective Abundance & Sunshine Souls

When you live as a radiant one in 5D, you don't just transform your personal life, you help rewire the collective field toward plenty.

Imagine more and more people releasing hoarding and competition because they feel genuinely safe in an abundant universe.

"Let's help each other" becomes the natural ethic. In such a climate, war, poverty, and greed lose fuel.

This is part of the ascension vision: resources shared wisely, needs met more easily, and a lived recognition that helping another is helping oneself, because *we are one*.

*A gentle clarification: higher teachings were never meant to shame material wellbeing or make poverty a virtue.

They free us from fear and attachment so prosperity can be received and stewarded with wisdom.

Live well in ways that honor your soul and do no harm to others. When you seek the kingdom within first, you actually become a better receiver: steady, joyful, and discerning.

As you practice radiating abundance, expect the "quiet magic" of synchronicity: a timely gift, unexpected income arriving when needed, support appearing from unlikely places.

Give thanks and let these moments strengthen trust. Over seasons, you gather not only faith but a tangible track record that spiritual principle produces material harmony, an embodied knowing that becomes part of your 5D mastery.

Remember: shifting from getting to radiating is the movement from a mindset of lack to a consciousness of abundance.

You are a powerful co-creator with Source, not a victim of circumstance. In 5D you don't pray in desperation, you pray in thanksgiving, resting in the awareness that it's already being taken care of.

You don't act from greed, you act from generosity and creativity, knowing there is always more flow.

Become a "sunshine soul": shine outward with quiet confidence that the universe supports you, the way a star is held in its galaxy.

Your light uplifts others; your grace encourages them. Infinite abundance is the truth of your being. Everything else was a temporary lesson.

# Chapter 21
## The Future Is Watching: Love Beyond Division

We are not only the descendants of those who came before, we are also the ancestors of those yet to come. The future looks back at us through the lens of our choices today. Some of what we call "extraterrestrial contact" is not contact with strangers at all but encounters with versions of ourselves from possible futures.

### Future Humans as Mirrors

Throughout history, there have been reports of luminous beings, radiant presences of light, who inspire awe, peace, and reverence. There have also been accounts of more clinical visitors, often described as grays, whose actions seem cold and detached. Both are human stories reflected across time.

The grays represent a path where intellect was chosen over empathy. In that trajectory, humanity survived but lost emotional depth, connection, and the ability to love fully. Now, they return in an attempt to recover what was lost, to reclaim the codes of love carried in our DNA.

The luminous beings embody a different possibility. They are humanity choosing the way of the heart: balance, unity, compassion, and Christ consciousness. They come not to save us, but to remind us: this is who you can become when love leads the way.

## Disclosure as Recognition

True disclosure is not a government announcement or a fleet appearing in the skies. It is the quiet recognition that these beings are our family, echoes of humanity's choices returning across time. They are not "other," but reflections of us. To see them rightly, we must first see ourselves rightly.

## Interventions and Warnings

There are moments when future humanity intervenes gently, especially around nuclear crises. These interventions are not about control but about keeping the door open to better timelines. A catastrophe once scarred their lineage, and they come with the plea: do not repeat this mistake.

## The Power of Choice

Every act of kindness, every choice for fear, every moment of compassion ripples forward. The way we treat a neighbor, a child, even ourselves, shapes both the sorrows and the radiance that may one day appear to us as visitors. The future is not a fixed script; it is a living field that bends to the frequencies we hold.

## Timelines and Ascension

Multiple realities co-exist. The frequency we maintain determines which version of Earth we experience. When we align with love, forgiveness, and service, we shift into gentler timelines. When we live in fear and division, we step into harsher ones. Ascension is the steady practice of choosing love until it becomes second nature, until the Christ Light within us shines without interruption.

## The Collective Vision

Imagine a world where enough of us live as radiant beings, secure in abundance, no longer hoarding or competing, but trusting in the infinite flow of Source. War, poverty, and greed would dissolve, not because they were conquered, but because they were starved of belief. This is the ascension vision: a humanity so luminous that our future selves return not in warning, but in celebration.

## **A Practical Invitation**

Ask yourself today:
- How am I living as an ancestor to the future?

- What choices am I making that ripple forward into generations I may one day meet?

- When I encounter "the other" — stranger, neighbor, or visitor — do I respond in fear or in love?

The future is watching. More truthfully, the future is being written through us, right now.

When we choose love, we are shaping the visitors of tomorrow into beings of light, not beings of lack.

# Appendix A

## *Sacred Echoes*

Across cultures and centuries, humanity has spoken to Source in story, poem, and prayer. Though time and translation have scattered these voices, they share a common resonance: love, trust, and belonging. In this appendix, we revisit ancient texts, not through the lens of dogma, but in the light of universal spirituality.

### •The Psalm of Trust (Psalm 23)

**Original Text**

The Lord is my shepherd; I shall not want...

**Universal Reframing**

The Lord is my shepherd.
Source is my guide.
I do not walk in lack, for love provides what I need.

Green pastures become symbols of rest.

Still waters remind me that peace flows quietly, endlessly.
When I feel scattered, love restores me.
When I feel lost, love leads me home.

The path is not mine alone to find.
It unfolds because Source has written goodness into the very fabric of being.
Even when shadows lengthen, even when the valley grows dark,
I need not fear.
For love walks beside me,
Comforting, steady, unshakable.

The table is always set.
Even when enemies surround me,
I discover abundance in the center of struggle.
Love anoints me, reminding me that I am more than dust and breath —
I am flame, I am spirit, I am beloved.

Surely goodness and mercy are not occasional visitors.
They are the ground beneath my feet.
They follow me, enfold me, go before me.
And I shall dwell — not in walls of stone, not in creeds, not in fear —
but in the vast house of Love,
Forever.

## Reflection

This psalm, cherished in Jewish and Christian traditions, is revealed as a universal hymn of trust. It reminds us that Source is not distant but present, restoring, guiding, and accompanying us in both abundance and trial.

## •Mesopotamian Wisdom

### Original Text

A loving heart builds houses. A hating heart destroys houses.

### Universal Reframing

Love creates shelter. Love makes room. Hate unravels the walls of belonging.

### Reflection

Even the oldest voices of civilization remind us that love builds what fear tears down.

## •Bhagavad Gita

### Original Text

Perform all actions with an even mind, abandoning attachment to success or failure. Such equanimity is yoga. (Gita 2:48)

### Universal Reframing

Do what is yours to do with steadiness of heart. Let go of outcomes, for peace is found not in winning, but in alignment.

**Reflection**

The Gita whispers that freedom is not in control but in surrender.

## •Tao Te Ching

**Original Text**

The Tao is like water. It benefits all things and does not compete. (Chapter 8)

**Universal Reframing**

Be like water — nourishing, yielding, unresisting. Love does not strive; it simply flows.

**Reflection**

In Daoist thought, as in every tradition, Source is gentle strength, flowing into all without division.

## •Dhammapada

### Original Text

Hatred does not cease by hatred, but only by love; this is the eternal rule. (Dhammapada 1:5)

### Universal Reframing

Anger cannot end anger. Only love softens the wound. This is the way it has always been.

### Reflection

The Buddha points to the same golden thread: division dissolves only in love.


## •Lakota Wisdom

### Original Text

Mitákuye Oyás'iŋ — we are all related.

### Universal Reframing

All beings are kin. The two-legged, the four-legged, the winged, the rooted — all belong.

### Reflection

The Lakota teaching of kinship affirms the same truth: spirituality without borders is the way of the earth itself.

## •Rumi (Sufi Tradition)

### Original Text

The wound is the place where the Light enters you.

### Universal Reframing

Even in pain, love seeps in. The cracks are not endings, but doorways.

### Reflection

Sufi mysticism teaches us that brokenness is a place of encounter with Source.

## •Upanishads

### Original Text

The Self is everywhere, shining forth from all beings. (Katha Upanishad 2.2.9)

### Universal Reframing

The light you seek is already within, gleaming in every face, burning in every heart.

### Reflection

The Upanishads proclaim unity: all beings reflect the same inner flame.

## •Navajo Blessing Way

### Original Text

In beauty may I walk. All day long may I walk.

### Universal Reframing

May I walk in beauty, step by step. May each breath remember harmony.

### Reflection

Indigenous wisdom affirms harmony with earth, spirit, and all relations.


## •Gospel of John

### Original Text

God is love, and those who abide in love abide in God. (1 John 4:16)

### Universal Reframing

Where love dwells, Source dwells. To live in love is to live in God.

### Reflection

Christianity at its essence speaks the same golden truth: love is the dwelling place of the Divine.

## •Ancient Egyptian (Book of the Dead)

### Original Text

I have not caused pain. I have not made anyone weep. I have not caused harm. (Negative Confessions)

### Universal Reframing

I choose the way of gentleness. I walk without causing harm. My legacy is kindness, not sorrow.

### Reflection

Ancient Egypt rooted righteousness in compassion — a reminder that love is justice lived out.

## •Stoic Philosophy (Marcus Aurelius)

### Original Text

Love the hand that fate deals you, and play it as your own. (Meditations 7.57)

### Universal Reframing

Embrace what comes. Even challenge carries love's imprint when we greet it with acceptance.

### Reflection

Stoicism and spirituality meet in surrender — trust that Source shapes every moment.

## •Mayan Prayer

**Original Text**

We are the maize people.

**Universal Reframing**

We are born of the earth's body, nourished by her grain, carried by her breath.

**Reflection**

The Mayan voice reminds us of our inseparability from the earth as kin.

## •Zoroastrian Text (Avesta)

**Original Text**

Good thoughts, good words, good deeds — this is the essence of the religion of Zarathustra.

**Universal Reframing**

Let the mind dwell on kindness, the tongue speak truth, the hands do love. Nothing else is required.

### Reflection

Zoroastrian wisdom centers on simplicity: love lived in thought, word, and deed.

## •Confucius (Analects)

### Original Text

Do not impose on others what you do not wish for yourself. (Analects 15.24)

### Universal Reframing

Treat each as you long to be treated. Respect is love in practice.

### Reflection

A principle that appears in nearly every tradition — proof that love's law is universal.

## •African Proverb (Akan, Ghana)

### Original Text

Wisdom is like a baobab tree; no one individual can embrace it.

### Universal Reframing

Truth is too vast for one alone. We must gather together, each with our hands, to hold it.

**Reflection**

African wisdom affirms that love and understanding grow in community, not isolation.

## •Native Hawaiian Chant (Hoʻoponopono Prayer)

**Original Text**

I am sorry. Please forgive me. Thank you. I love you.

**Universal Reframing**

In humility I return. In forgiveness I am restored. In gratitude, I open. In love I am whole.

**Reflection**

Hawaiian practice reminds us that reconciliation and healing flow through love.

## •Rabindranath Tagore

### Original Text

I slept and dreamt that life was joy. I awoke and saw that life was service. I acted and behold, service was joy.

### Universal Reframing

Joy is not only given but lived. In serving, I awaken. In awakening, I rejoice.

### Reflection

Tagore bridges East and West, showing that love becomes joy when embodied in service.


## •Hafiz

### Original Text

I wish I could show you, when you are lonely or in darkness, the astonishing light of your own being.

### Universal Reframing

Even in your darkest night, you shine. Love's light is within you, waiting to be seen.

### Reflection

Hafiz sings that the Divine is not apart from us, but radiates through us.

## •Nelson Mandela

**Original Text**

No one is born hating another person because of the color of his skin... People must learn to hate, and if they can learn to hate, they can be taught to love.

**Universal Reframing**

Love is our first language. Hatred is only learned — and it can be unlearned. Love waits to be remembered.

**Reflection**

Mandela reminds us that love is humanity's native ground, stronger than fear or prejudice.

## Closing Reflection

Across scriptures, poems, prayers, and teachings, the same current runs: love is not bound to one religion, time, or people.

It is the voice of Source, singing through the human heart in every age.

Christ consciousness, Buddha nature, the Tao, the Great Spirit, all point to the same inner light, reminding us of who we are and what we share.

As we listen to these sacred echoes, may we realize that humanity has always known the truth:
we are one family, born of one Source, destined for one homecoming in love.

Love is the way.

Love has always been the way.

Love will forever be the way.

## Journaling with Sacred Echoes

Take a few quiet moments to reflect on the universal wisdom carried through these sacred echoes.
Use the prompts below to deepen your personal connection to the truths they reveal.

- Which passage or tradition in this appendix resonated most deeply with me? Why?

- How does hearing the same truth of love across cultures affect my understanding of Source?

- In what ways have I already experienced this universal current of love in my own life?




- How might I live more consciously as a "sacred echo" of love in my family, community, or world?

- If I were to leave one echo of love for future generations, what words would I offer?




Write from the heart, without editing or judgment.

Let the echoes of love in these traditions call forth the echo within you.

# Appendix B

## The Psalm of Trust:

## A Universal Reframing

Across cultures and centuries, humanity has spoken to Source in story, poem, and prayer. Though time and translation have scattered these voices, they share a common resonance: love, trust, and belonging. In this appendix, we revisit ancient texts, not through the lens of dogma, but in the light of universal spirituality.

Sacred texts often carry truths deeper than the boundaries of any one tradition. The Psalm of Trust is one such treasure, echoing across centuries in words first spoken within a particular culture but resonating universally.

When read through the lens of Source and unity, it becomes not a creed of exclusivity but a hymn for all humanity. Here is a reframing of the beloved Psalm 23, revealing its timeless wisdom as a guide for trust in Love itself.

## The Psalm of Trust: A Universal Reframing

The Lord is my shepherd.
Source is my guide.
I do not walk in lack, for love provides what I need.

Green pastures become symbols of rest.
Still waters remind me that peace flows quietly, endlessly.
When I feel scattered, love restores me.
When I feel lost, love leads me home.

The path is not mine alone to find.
It unfolds because Source has written goodness into the very fabric of being.
Even when shadows lengthen, even when the valley grows dark,
I need not fear.
For love walks beside me,
comforting, steady, unshakable.

The table is always set.
Even when enemies surround me,
I discover abundance in the center of struggle.
Love anoints me, reminding me that I am more than dust

and breath —
I am flame, I am spirit, I am beloved.

Surely goodness and mercy are not occasional visitors.
They are the ground beneath my feet.
They follow me, enfold me, go before me.
And I shall dwell — not in walls of stone, not in creeds, not in fear —
but in the vast house of Love,
forever.

## Closing Reflection

At its heart, the Psalm of Trust is a reminder that Source never abandons, never withholds, and never ceases to guide us.
Green pastures and still waters are metaphors for the peace available when we align with love.
The table of abundance is set for all, not a select few.
Even shadows hold no terror when we know the Presence walks with us.
Trust is not passive; it is the daily practice of remembering that Love sustains and leads us in every circumstance.
This reframing reveals that the psalm's comfort belongs not to one people, but to every soul who dares to trust Love.

## Journaling with the Psalm of Trust

Use these prompts to help you engage personally with the Psalm of Trust and its universal message.

- Where in my life have I felt Source leading me beside "still waters" or restoring my soul?

- How do I experience abundance already present in my daily life?

- What shadows am I walking through now, and how might I invite Love to guide me without fear?

- What does it mean to me to "dwell in the house of Love" here and now?

- How can I live as a living psalm of trust — radiating peace, abundance, and courage to others?

Write from the heart, and let trust rise in you as both comfort and strength.

# Epilogue

## Remembering Love

As humanity awakens from the long dream of separation, we are beginning to remember that God was never distant, and love was never withheld. The Infinite has always been here, not in temples or texts alone, but within every breath, every heart, every act of kindness and courage.

Love and faith are not opposites. They are companions on the same journey, one revealing the other. Faith opens the heart to love's guidance; love gives faith its meaning. Together they become the bridge that carries us beyond religion, beyond fear, and into unity with all life.

You do not need to strive for enlightenment or chase spiritual perfection. Simply be willing to love; to see through the eyes of compassion, to listen with patience, to forgive without conditions. In that willingness, the Divine remembers Itself through you.

May you walk forward in peace, awake to the beauty of your own soul, and certain that love was always the truth behind it all.

# Closing Blessing

May the light within you rise to meet the dawn.
May your heart remember what the mind forgets;
that you are, and have always been, one with Love.

May your faith no longer rest in fear or form,
but in the quiet knowing that the Infinite walks beside
you, within you, and through you in every breath.

May your path be soft beneath your feet,
your words be kind,
and your presence be a balm to those you meet.

And when doubt whispers,
may you turn inward and feel the steady pulse of Love
reminding you, you are home, you are whole,
you are the living expression of the Divine.

Go in peace, dear soul.
Live in love, walk in faith,
and remember —
you were never separate from Source.

www.ingramcontent.com/pod-product-compliance
Lightning Source LLC
Chambersburg PA
CBHW020854090426
42736CB00008B/372